Chinese *with* Mike

Addictive learning

Advanced Beginner to Intermediate Activity Book

Professor Mike Hainzinger

First published in Great Britain in 2015 by Hodder and Stoughton.
An Hachette UK company.

Copyright © Mike Hainzinger 2015

The right of Mike Hainzinger to be identified as the Author of the Work
has been asserted by him in accordance with the Copyright, Designs and
Patents Act 1988.

CHINESE WITH MIKE™ is a trademark of Language Moves, LLC.

Database right Hodder & Stoughton (makers)

The *Teach Yourself* name is a registered trademark of Hachette UK.

British Library Cataloguing in Publication Data: a catalogue record for this
title is available from the British Library.

Library of Congress Catalogue Card Number: on file.

9781444198607

The publisher has used its best endeavours to ensure that any website
addresses referred to in this book are correct and active at the time
of going to press. However, the publisher and the author have no
responsibility for the websites and can make no guarantee that a site will
remain live or that the content will remain relevant, decent or appropriate.

The publisher has made every effort to mark as such all words which it
believes to be trademarks. The publisher should also like to make it clear
that the presence of a word in the book, whether marked or unmarked,
in no way affects its legal status as a trademark.

Every reasonable effort has been made by the publisher to trace the
copyright holders of material in this book. Any errors or omissions should
be notified in writing to the publisher, who will endeavour to rectify the
situation for any reprints and future editions.

Typeset by Graphicraft Limited, Hong Kong.

Printed and bound in Great Britain by CPI Group (UK) Ltd, Croydon CR0 4YY

John Murray Learning policy is to use papers that are natural, renewable
and recyclable products and made from wood grown in sustainable forests.
The logging and manufacturing processes are expected to conform to
the environmental regulations of the country of origin.

John Murray Learning
Carmelite House
50 Victoria Embankment
London EC4Y 0DZ
www.hodder.co.uk

Voice credits:
Recorded at Alchemy Studios, London.
Cast: Sarah Cole, Xiaoyun Yao, Qiang Wu

Contents

Introduction

Welcome to the **Advanced Beginner to Intermediate Activity Book** for *Chinese with Mike*. This book should be used in conjunction with the corresponding audio and with the **Advanced Beginner to Intermediate Coursebook** and videos.

Chinese with Mike consists of training in listening, speaking, reading, and writing in Mandarin Chinese. Each level is composed of videos, coursebooks, and activity books that together provide a comprehensive system for learning Chinese. **Advanced Beginner to Intermediate**, contains Season 3 (*Lessons 61–80*), Season 4 (*Lessons 81–100*) and Season 5 (*Lessons 101–120*) of *Chinese with Mike*. Each lesson comprises a 10–15 minute video, a corresponding lesson in both the **Coursebook** and **Activity Book**, lots of activities in a variety of types, and supplemental audio.

The **Activity Book** expands the lessons from the corresponding **Coursebook**, providing additional practice for each of the sixty **Advanced Beginner to Intermediate** lessons.

While the **Coursebook** focuses on presenting vocabulary and language functions you need, the **Activity Book** gives you a workout in elementary reading and writing as well as in comprehension and speaking.

Most of all, the **Activity Book** serves as the listening component for the course and the supplemental audio includes beginner conversations and exercises spoken by native speakers that will let you hone your listening and speaking skills.

Activity types are designated by icons. Here is a list:

 audio/listening icon

 reading icon

 speaking icon

 Internet activity

 video icon

How to Use This Book

In *Chinese with Mike* you will learn Mandarin Chinese through **pīnyīn**, a romanization system that will help you understand and pronounce Mandarin characters through the ABC alphabet you already know. By using the many exercises in pronunciation, recognition, and discrimination of sounds, tones, and spelling provided in the first eight lessons you can build a solid foundation in Mandarin that is guaranteed to speed your progress through the entire course. Take your time and go over and over these beginning listening and pronunciation activities – it's a great investment and your time will not be wasted!

When you do **speaking** activities, be sure to speak and speak out loud! An extra little tip: Record your voice so you can hear yourself and compare your pronunciation with native speakers on the audio. You might also keep a log and track sounds you are having difficulty with or sounds that you are quite good at reproducing. This can be a written log and/or an audio log. With an audio log you'll be able to hear how far you have come by the end of the course.

For **listening activities**, a special note: Always listen to a passage many times! "Gap" activities ask you to listen for certain information in a sentence or passage; these activities will sharpen your ability to recognize words by hearing alone. In addition, several of the conversations are intended to be read as you listen and this will help you match the sounds of your new language to the words you are reading. Thus the listening exercises can help you learn to read pīnyīn as well as understand spoken Chinese.

Reading exercises offer an introduction to basic **character** recognition and elementary reading from basic word level to elementary sentence level.

Throughout the course, I suggest you keep a notebook. Jot down patterns or points that are especially difficult and examples that illustrate how it should be done and should *not* be done.

Lastly, taking on a language is a big task, and there are bound to be times when you feel discouraged. However, I'll be your guide along the way and will provide encouragement and keep you going as you take your first steps into Mandarin.

Yǒu

A Write the name of the new vocabulary word under its corresponding picture.

1 (John) 2 (Yasmina) 3 (Tom) 4 (Lily) 5 (Amy) 6 (Lisa)

_____ _____ _____ _____ _____ _____

B Using your answers for 1–6, create questions or answers about what these people have.

1 John yǒu shénme?

John _____.

2 Yasmina yǒu shénme?

Yasmina _____.

3 Tom yǒu shénme?

Tom _____.

4 Lily _____?

Lily yǒu bǐjìběn diànnǎo.

5 Amy yǒu shénme?

Amy _____.

6 Lisa _____?

Lisa yǒu yōupán.

 C 61.01 Listen and complete the following sentences. When you are done, listen to the audio again and repeat the sentences out loud, paying close attention to tone and pronunciation.

1 Tā xiǎng mǎi _____.

2 Xuéshēng yǒu Zhōngwén _____.

3 Nà shì hěn guìde _____.

4 Wǒ māma hěn xǐhuān _____.

5 Zhè shì lánsède _____.

6 Mèimei xǐhuān tāde xīnde _____.

D Read the conversation and answer the questions.

Dàwèi:	Nǐ xiǎng mǎi shénme?
Pèishān:	Wǒ xiǎng mǎi píngbǎn diànnǎo.
Dàwèi:	Wǒ yǒu píngbǎn diànnǎo. Píngbǎn diànnǎo hěn hǎoyòng.
Pèishān:	Xiànzài wǒ yòng bǐjìběn diànnǎo, dànshì wǒde bǐjìběn diànnǎo hěn jiù.
Dàwèi:	Wǒ mèimei xiǎng mǎi bǐjìběn diànnǎo. Nǐ yào bú yào mài nǐde?
Pèishān:	Yào.
Dàwèi:	Duōshǎo qián?
Pèishān:	Bābǎi yuán
Dàwèi:	Hǎo. Nǐ yào bú yào tāde diànhuà hàomǎ?
Pèishān:	Yào. Xièxie!

1 What would Pèishān like to buy?

2 Why does Pèishān want to sell her laptop computer?

3 Who might want to buy Pèishān's laptop computer?

4 How much money does Pèishān want for her laptop computer?

Méi Yǒu

A Match the new vocabulary words with their definitions.

1 ___ làbǐ   **a** chalk

2 ___ fěnbǐ   **b** brush pen

3 ___ shūbāo   **c** crayon

4 ___ máobǐ   **d** marker; marker pen

5 ___ mǎkèbǐ   **e** a camera

6 ___ qiānbǐ   **f** a bookbag

7 ___ (zhào)xiàngjī   **g** a pencil

B Unscramble the words to make sentences with "yǒu".

1 méi / yǒu / shūbāo / wǒ _____

2 ma / yǒu / nǐde / lǎoshī / mǎkèbǐ _____

3 Tàitai / yǒu / méi / Lǐ / xiàngjī _____

4 yǒu / nánpéngyǒu / ma / nǐde / qiānbǐ _____

C Use the words in parentheses to answer the questions with long answers.

Ex: Tāmen yǒu bǐjìběn diànnǎo ma? (no) → Méi yǒu. Tāmen méi yǒu bǐjìběn diànnǎo.

1 Nǐde xiǎoháizi yǒu shénme? (crayons) _____

2 Mike Lǎoshī yǒu hóngsède mǎkèbǐ ma? (no) _____

3 Xuéshēng yào bú yào mǎi Zhōngwén zìdiǎn? (yes) _____

4 Mèimeide shūbāo shì shénme yánsè? (pink) _____

5 Yéyede máobǐ hěn jiù ma? (yes) _____

6 Nǐde zhàoxiàngjī guì bú guì? (expensive) _____

D Some sentences contain errors with "bù / méi". Correct the errors if there are any.

Ex: Tā jiějie bù yǒu hóngsède huā. → (Incorrect) méi

1 Nǐmen yǒu fěnbǐ ma? Bù yǒu. _____

2 Nà shì méi shì nǐde hēisède shūbāo? _____

3 Wǒ érzi bú huì kāichē. _____

4 Zhè shì bú shì nǐde jiā? _____

E 62.01 **Complete the sentences with "yǒu / méi yǒu" and the noun that follows.**

1 Tāde nánpéngyǒu _____.

2 Nǐde nǚpéngyǒu _____.

3 Wǒ _____.

4 Tāmende lǎoshī _____.

Review Of Yǒu And Méi Yǒu

A **Match the words with their definitions.**

1 _____ diànhuà
2 _____ zhìnéng kǎ
3 _____ chōngdiànqì
4 _____ shǒujī
5 _____ zhìnéng shǒujī
6 _____ shǒujīké

a battery charger (for phones, computer, etc.)
b cell / mobile phone case
c smartphone
d cell phone / mobile
e a telephone
f a smart card; SIM card

B **Given the answer, write the corresponding question(s).**

Ex: A: Yǒu. Wǒ yǒu fěnhóngsède shǒujī. → **Q:** Nǐ yǒu fěnhóngsède shǒujī ma?
Nǐ yǒu méi yǒu fěnhóngsède shǒujī?

1 **A:** Méi yǒu. Wǒde péngyǒu méi yǒu zhìnéng kǎ. **Q:** _____
2 **A:** Yǒu. Tā yǒu zhìnéng shǒujī. **Q:** _____
3 **A:** Wǒde shǒujī shì huīsè. **Q:** _____
4 **A:** Chōngdiànqì 150 yuán. **Q:** _____

C **Locate the errors in the following sentences and rewrite them correctly.**

Ex: Wǒmende nǎinai bù yǒu diànnǎo. → Wǒmende nǎinai (méi) yǒu diànnǎo.

1 Nà shì shéide zhìnéng shǒujī ma? _____
2 Tā yào méi yào mǎi chōngdiànqì? _____
3 Nǐ xǐhuān wǒde shǒujīké? _____
4 Tāde diànhuà pián bú piányí? _____

D **Answer the following questions with long answers.**

Ex: Xuéshēng yǒu bǐjìběn ma? (Yes) → Yǒu. Xuéshēng yǒu bǐjìběn.

1 Nǐ yǒu nǐde qiānbǐ ma? (Yes) _____
2 Lǎoshī yǒu méi yǒu báisède fěnbǐ? (No) _____
3 Shéi yǒu chōngdiànqì? (Lily) _____
4 Nǐ yǒu méi yǒu hěn piányíde shǒujī? (Yes) _____

E "Míngtiān shì nǐ(de) péngyǒude shēngrì!" Using your vocabulary words from this lesson and the previous one, make a list of presents you might want to buy for your brother or sister, or friend. Don't worry about the cost!

Ex: zhìnéng shǒujī (a smartphone); (zhào)xiàngjī (a camera)

1 _____

2 _____

3 _____

4 _____

5 _____

6 _____

7 _____

8 _____

Hěn Duō

A **Choose the right word to complete the sentence.**

1 A hammer is a **mùgōng / chuízi**.

2 A drill is a **jìgōng / diànzuān**.

3 A saw is a **jùzi / luósīdāo**.

4 A carpenter is a **mùgōng / jìgōng**.

5 A mechanic is a **jìgōng / gōngjù**.

6 A wrench is a **qiánzi / bānshǒu**.

B **Negate the following statements.**

Ex: Zhè shì chuízi. → Zhè bú shì chuízi.

1 Wǒ yào yòng wǒde luósīdāo. _____

2 Tāmen yǒu hěn duō diànzuān. _____

3 Wǒ gēge shì jìgōng. _____

4 Mùgōng yǒu qiánzi. _____

C **Given the answer, write the question.**

Ex: A: Méi yǒu. Wǒmen méi yǒu hěn duō gōngjù. → **Q:** Nǐmen yǒu hěn duō gōngjù ma?
Nǐmen yǒu méi yǒu hěn duō gōngjù?

1 **A:** Xǐhuān. Wǒ bàba hěn xǐhuān tāde xīnde diànzuān. **Q:** _____

2 **A:** Bù xiǎng. Mùgōng bù xiǎng mài tāde jiùde gōngjù. **Q:** _____

3 **A:** Yǒu. Jìgōng yǒu hěn duō bānshǒu. **Q:** _____

4 **A:** Méi yǒu. Jìgōng méi yǒu jùzi. **Q:** _____

5 **A:** Nǐde gōngjù zài zhè lǐ. **Q:** _____

6 **A:** Bù. Wǒ(de) xiānshēngde gōngjùxiāng bú dà. **Q:** _____

D Let's bring this lesson to a close by looking over some vocabulary from past units. Check out the words in the word bank and place them into the following categories.

| qiánzi | shūbāo | luósīdāo | diànzuān | bǐjìběn diànnǎo | kèběn | qiānbǐ |
| (zhào)xiàngjī | jùzi | chōngdiànqì | zìdiǎn | shǒujī | chuízi |

Tools	School supplies	Electronic devices

E Decide whether these statements are true or false.

> Yīnwèi wǒ bàba shì mùgōng, suǒyǐ tā yǒu hěn dàde gōngjùxiāng, yě yǒu hěn duō hěn bàngde gōngjù. Wǒ bàba yǒu hěn duō chuízi, yě yǒu hěn duō luósīdāo. Tā yǒu hěn duō jùzi, dànshì tā méi yǒu hěn duō diànzuān. Tā yě méi yǒu hěn duō bānshǒu. Wǒ bàba méi yǒu qiánzi.

1 My dad is a mechanic.

2 My dad has a lot of tools.

3 My dad has a small toolbox.

4 My dad has a lot of hammers, screwdrivers, and drills.

5 My dad doesn't have a lot of wrenches and saws.

6 My dad doesn't have any pliers.

Measure Words

A **Translate these phrases into English.**

Ex: sìgè yáyī → four dentists

1 liǎnggè nǚ'ér _____

2 sāngè nánrén _____

3 yīgè háizi _____

4 shígè Zhōngguórén _____

5 wǔgè xiāofángyuán _____

6 liùgè Měiguórén _____

B **Now answer these yes / no questions with long answers. Translate the numbers into Chinese.**

Ex: Nǐ yǒu xiǎohái ma?   (Yes; 6) → Yǒu. Wǒ yǒu liùgè xiǎohái.

1 Nǐ yǒu érzi ma?   (Yes; 2) _____

2 Tā yǒu méi yǒu nǚ'ér?   (Yes; 3) _____

3 Tāmen yǒu xiǎohái ma?   (No) _____

4 Lǎoshī yǒu hěn duō xuéshēng ma?   (Yes; 25) _____

5 Nǐ gēge yǒu hěn duō péngyǒu ma?   (No) _____

6 Tā yǒu méi yǒu xiōngdì jiěmèi?   (No) _____

C **Unscramble the sentences. Use Chinese words for numerals. Some answers may have more than one correct answer.**

1 wǒmen / bóbo / yǒu / gè / 5 _____

2 lǎobǎn / 2 / mìshū / gè / yǒu _____

3 yīshēng / yīyuàn / yǒu / 13 / gè _____

4 yǒu / gè / 3 / wǒ / gēge _____

D **Translate the following English statements into Chinese.**

1 My girlfriend has four older sisters. _____

2 His dad has two younger brothers. _____

3 The professor doesn't have many students. _____

4 My daughter has three friends. _____

E Are these translations correct? Correct the incorrect sentences.

Ex: Tāde yáyī yǒu hěn xiǎode diànzuān. → His / Her dentist has a very small drill. (Correct)

1 Wǒ wàigōng yǒu hěn duō qián. My (maternal) grandfather has a lot of money.

_____

2 Tā méi yǒu nǐde chuízi. He / She has your hammer.

_____

3 Xiāofángyuán huì yòng hěn duō gōngjù. Firefighters know how to use many tools.

_____

4 Zhèxiē xiǎohái yǒu méi yǒu wánjù? These children don't have toys.

_____

5 Shéi yǒu bǐ? Who wants a pen?

_____

Jǐgè

A Choose the word that makes the most sense for each of the following sentences.

1 Wǒde **jìmǔ / jìfù** hěn piàoliàng.

2 Tāmende **jìfù / nǚ'ér** hěn shuài.

3 Wǒmende **érzi / jìfù** bā suì.

4 Nǐde **jìmǔ / nǚ'ér** shì xiǎoháizi. Tā bú huì kāichē.

B Given the answer, write the question.

Ex: A: Wǒde péngyǒu yǒu liǎnggè nǚ'ér. → **Q:** Nǐde péngyǒu yǒu jǐgè nǚ'ér?

1 **Q:** _____

A: Cāntīng yǒu liǎnggè chúshī.

2 **Q:** _____

A: Tāmen yǒu yīgè jiàoliàn.

3 **Q:** _____

A: Lín Tàitai yǒu sìgè xiǎohái.

4 **Q:** _____

A: Tā méi yǒu xiōngdì jiěmèi.

C Unscramble the sentences.

1 yǒu / tāmen / xiōngdi / jǐgè / ? _____

2 wǒde / jìfù / gōngzuò / zài _____

3 jìmǔ / tāde / shénme / jiào / míngzi / ? _____

4 méi / yǒu / Lily / yǒu / zìdiǎn / Yīngwén / ? _____

D Answer the questions using the words in parentheses.

Ex: Nǐde nánpéngyǒu yǒu hěn duō gōngjù ma? (No) →
   Méi yǒu. Wǒde nánpéngyǒu méi yǒu hěn duō gōngjù.

1 Tā yǒu nǚpéngyǒu ma? (No) _____

2 Tā yǒu méi yǒu dìdi? (Yes; 2) _____

3 Tā yǒu gēge ma? (Yes; 1) _____

4 Tāde bàbamāma yǒu hěn dàde fángzi ma? (No) _____

E Translate the following sentences.

1 Tā shì yīgè shāngrén. _____

2 Lǎoshī yǒu shíwùgè xuéshēng. _____

3 Nǐ yǒu jǐgè péngyǒu? _____

4 Zhè shì shéide shǒujī? _____

F Look at the family tree. Pretend you are Alexander. Say who you are and explain who your family is.

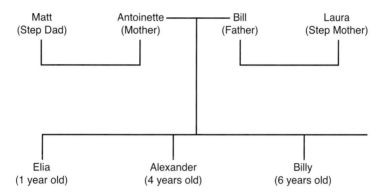

More Measure Words

A **Match the words and definitions.**

1 ___ jǐ
2 ___ nóngchǎng
3 ___ gè
4 ___ chǒngwù
5 ___ kǒu
6 ___ chǒngwùdiàn
7 ___ zhī
8 ___ běn

a a pet store
b how many
c a farm
d MW for books, magazines, book-like objects
e MW for animals
f MW for people, general objects
g a house pet
h MW for people (fml)

B **Look at the drawing then answer the questions in Mandarin.**

(Lily)

1 Where is Lily? _____

2 How is the weather? _____

3 How many goats does she have? _____

4 How many chickens does she have? _____

5 Does she have a cat? If so, how many? _____

6 Is her dog big or little? _____

C Write long answers using the numbers in parentheses.

Ex: Tāmen yǒu jǐgè háizi? (3) → Tāmen yǒu sāngè háizi.

1 Nǐ yǒu jǐběn Zhōngwén kèběn? (2) _____

2 Nóngchǎng yǒu jǐzhī yāzi? (14) _____

3 Nǐmen jiā yǒu jǐzhī māo? (4) _____

4 Xuéxiào yǒu jǐgè lǎoshī? (27) _____

D Read the answer and write out the corresponding question using "jǐ" and a measure word.

Ex: A: Wǒ yào mǎi liǎngběn Rìwén kèběn.   **Q:** Nǐ yào mǎi jǐběn Rìwén kèběn?

1 A: Tā(de) jiā yǒu liùkǒu rén.   **Q:** _____

2 A: Chǒngwùdiàn yǒu bāzhī māo.   **Q:** _____

3 A: Nóngchǎng yǒu shízhī jī.   **Q:** _____

4 A: Cāntīng yǒu liǎnggè chúshī.   **Q:** _____

5 A: Tā yǒu sānběn Fǎwén shū.   **Q:** _____

Even More Measure Words

A Choose the word that best completes each sentence.

1 **Qǐng / Píng** gěi wǒ yībēi chéngzhī.

2 Wǒ yào hē yībēi **pútáojiǔ / píngzi**.

3 Wǒ xiǎng qù jiǔbā hē **píjiǔ / hóngchá**.

4 Míngtiān māma yào qù mǎi yī **zhāng / gè** chuáng.

5 Nǐmende **lǜchá / fěnbǐ** hǎo bù hǎohē?

6 Shéi xiǎng hē **xiāngbīnjiǔ / jiǔbā**?

B Fill in the beverage menu with the words in the word bank.

| píjiǔ | píngguǒzhī | chéngzhī | hóngchá | hóngpútáojiǔ |
| lǜchá | xiāngbīnjiǔ | báipútáojiǔ | níngméngzhī |

Beverages

Alcoholic beverages	Teas	Juices

C Put the correct measure word for each group of nouns.

Ex: dìdi, jiějie, nánpéngyǒu, lǎogōng → (gè)

1 _____ jī, gǒu, niǎo, māo

2 _____ liànxíběn, zázhì, kèběn, shū

3 _____ zhuōzi, yǐzi, zhǐ, chuáng

4 _____ pútáojiǔ, xiāngbīnjiǔ, shuǐ, niúnǎi

5 _____ Déguórén, Yìdàlìrén, Yīngguórén

6 _____ shāngrén, nóngmín, yǎnyuán

D Given the answer, write the question.

Ex: **A:** Wǒ yǒu liǎngpíng píjiǔ. → **Q:** Nǐ yǒu jǐpíng píjiǔ?

1 **A:** Xiǎng. Wǒmen xiǎng hē yībēi lǜchá.   **Q:** _____

2 **A:** Méi yǒu. Wǒ méi yǒu hóngchá.   **Q:** _____

3 **A:** Xǐhuān. Wǒ mán xǐhuān hē pútáojiǔ.   **Q:** _____

4 **A:** Bù kěyǐ. Tāde érzi bù kěyǐ hē kāfēi.   **Q:** _____

5 **A:** Tāmen yǒu sìběn Xībānyáwén shū.   **Q:** _____

6 **A:** Yǒu. Nóngmín yǒu wǔzhī jī.   **Q:** _____

E Change affirmative-negative questions to "ma" questions.

Ex: Nǐ yào bú yào hē xiāngbīnjiǔ? → Nǐ yào hē xiāngbīnjiǔ ma?

1 Tā xǐ bù xǐhuān hē hóngpútáojiǔ? _____

2 Nǐmen jiā yǒu méi yǒu chá? _____

3 Nǐ néng bù néng bāng wǒ mǎi liǎngpíng báipútáojiǔ? _____

4 Tāmen xiǎng bù xiǎng mǎi yīpíng shuǐ? _____

Zhègè vs. Nàgè

A Sort these words into two groups: people and places.

gāozhōngshēng	nánhái(zi)	nǚrén	gāozhōng	nánrén
dàxué	dàxuéshēng	nǚhái(zi)	xuéxiào	

People	Places

B Using the people and places in the table above, make up sentences about where the following people are. You may use the "place" words more than once. Then translate them into English.

Ex. Nàgè nánrén zài dàxué. → That man is at the university.

1 _____

2 _____

3 _____

4 _____

C Unscramble these sentences, and when you're done, translate them into English.

1 fēicháng / gāozhōngshēng / nàgè / gāo _____

2 xiānshēng / nǚrénde / zhègè / yáyī / shì _____

3 nàgè / xǐhuān / bù / píjiǔ / hē / dàxuéshēng _____

4 hěn / jǐngchá / zhègè / qínláo _____

D Choose the answer that makes sense based on the people's ages.

Ex: Stephen sānshí suì. Tā shì **nánrén** / (**nánháizi**).

1 Lily shíwǔ suì. Tā shì **gāozhōngshēng** / **dàxuéshēng**.

2 Thomas èrshí suì. Tā shì **nánháizi** / **dàxuéshēng**.

3 Benjamin qī suì. Tā shì **nánháizi** / **nánrén**.

4 Charlotte liù suì. Tā shì **nǚháizi** / **nǚrén**.

E Given the answers, write the questions.

Ex: A: Nàgè nǚrén shì wǒ māma. → **Q:** Nàgè nǚrén shì shéi?

1 A: Xǐhuān. Wǒ xǐhuān zhègè lǎoshī.

Q: _____

2 A: Méi yǒu. Nàgè nánrén méi yǒu fángzi.

Q: _____

3 A: Huì. Zhègè gāozhōngshēng huì qí mótuōchē.

Q: _____

4 A: Bù. Nàgè nánháizi bù guāi.

Q: _____

5 A: Shì. Zhègè nǚrén shì wǒde āyí.

Q: _____

Zhè / Nà And Other Measure Words

A Use the vocabulary to provide adjectives for the following objects.

tàng	cháng	bīng	zhòng	yìng	ruǎn

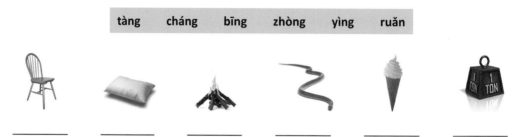

_____   _____   _____   _____   _____   _____

B Some of the following sentences contain the wrong MW. Give the correct MW for each sentence and then translate the whole sentence into English.

Ex: Nàzhāng nǚháizi shì wǒde nǚ'ér. → (gè) That girl is my daughter.

1 Zhèpíng xiāngbīnjiǔ hěn guì. _____

2 Nàbēi xióng hěn dà. _____

3 Wǒ yào mǎi wǔzhī tùzi. _____

4 Mèimei xiǎng hē yīzhāng chéngzhī. _____

5 Nàzhāng yǐzi shì shéide? _____

6 Nàběn zázhì hěn hǎokàn. _____

C Translate these phrases into Chinese.

Ex: this Chinese textbook → zhèběn Zhōngwén kèběn

1 that lion _____

2 that comfortable bed _____

3 this cup of coffee _____

4 that French book _____

5 this bowl of soup _____

6 this high school student _____

D Unscramble the sentences. Remember to look for clues as to whether a sentence is a question or a statement.

1 nà / tùzi / zhī / de / cháng / ěrduō / hěn _____

2 nánpéngyǒu / ma / nàgè / tāde / rén / shì _____

3 Xiǎoxin! / tāng / zhè / hěn / tàng / wǎn _____

4 yīnwèi / shǒu / wǒde / bīng / hěn / suǒyǐ / dài / yào / wǒ / shǒutào _____

5 běn / kèběn / bú / guì / guì / Rìwén / zhè _____

Prepositions 1

A Give the meanings of your new vocabulary words.

1 wàiguórén _____

2 lóushàng _____

3 lǐmiàn _____

4 wàimiàn _____

5 fángjiān _____

6 lóuxià _____

B Given the answer, write the question.

Ex: A: Bú zài. Bàba bú zài lǐmiàn. → **Q:** Bàba zài lǐmiàn ma?

1 A: Zài. Dìdi zài tāde fángjiān.

　　Q: _____

2 A: Bú zài. Wǒ bú zài wàimiàn.

　　Q: _____

3 A: Wǒmen zài lóuxià.

　　Q: _____

4 A: Wǒde fángjiān zài lóushàng.

　　Q: _____

C Unscramble the following sentences.

Ex: zài / shéi / wàimiàn? → Shéi zài wàimiàn?

1 lǎogōng / nǐde / shì / wàiguórén / bú / shì / ? _____

2 zài / nǐde / māo / lóushàng / ma / ? _____

3 jiějiede / fángjiān / zài / nǎ lǐ / nǐ / ? _____

4 nánpéngyǒu / tāde / lóuxià / zài _____

D **Status updates: Where are the following people? Translate the following social media updates from Chinese to English.**

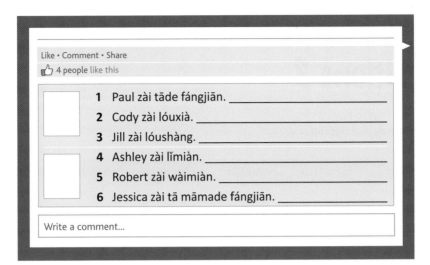

Like • Comment • Share

👍 4 people like this

1 Paul zài tāde fángjiān. _____

2 Cody zài lóuxià. _____

3 Jill zài lóushàng. _____

4 Ashley zài lǐmiàn. _____

5 Robert zài wàimiàn. _____

6 Jessica zài tā māmade fángjiān. _____

Write a comment...

Prepositions 2

A Match the words and definitions.

qiángbì	qiánmiàn	hòumiàn	shàngmiàn	xiàmiàn	lǐmiàn

1 above _____

2 behind _____

3 in front of _____

4 wall _____

5 under _____

6 inside _____

B Answer the questions using the words in parentheses.

Ex: Nǐmende péngyǒu zài nǎ lǐ? (in front of the convenience store) →
Wǒmende péngyǒu zài biànlì shāngdiànde qiánmiàn.

1 Bēizi zài nǎ lǐ? (on the table) _____

2 Nǐde bǐjìběn diànnǎo zài nǎ lǐ? (in my bookbag) _____

3 Bàbade chuízi zài nǎ lǐ? (in the toolbox) _____

4 Dìdide zāngde yīfú zài nǎ lǐ? (under his bed) _____

5 Jiàoshòu zài nǎ lǐ? (behind you) _____

C Translate the following sentences into Chinese. Don't forget your measure words.

Ex: She is behind the tree. → Tā zài shùde hòumiàn.

1 The monkeys are at the zoo. _____

2 This book is on the chair. _____

3 That cat is under the table. _____

4 Four oranges are in the refrigerator. _____

5 His dinner is in the oven. _____

6 I am in the living room. _____

7 The clock is on the wall. _____

8 The TV is in front of the wall. _____

    1 Xiànzài Dàwèi zài nǎ lǐ?

        Xiànzài Dàwèi zài _____.

    2 Zuótiān Pèishān zài nǎ lǐ?

        Zuótiān Pèishān zài tāde _____.

    3 Xīngqīliù Dàwèi zài nǎ lǐ?

        Xīngqīliù Dàwèi zài cāntīngde _____.

    4 Qiántiān Pèishān zài nǎ lǐ?

        Qiántiān Pèishān zài _____.

    5 Xīngqīrì Dàwèi zài nǎ lǐ?

        Xīngqīrì Dàwèi zài _____.

    6 Jīntiān Pèishān zài nǎ lǐ?

        Jīntiān Pèishān zài túshūguǎnde _____.

E **Go to your favorite room in your house. Describe your surroundings. Use prepositions to talk about where people / things are located in the room.**

    Ex: Wǒ zài kètīng. Shízhōng zài qiángbì shàng. Diànshì zài qiángbìde qiánmiàn . . .
        (I am in the living room. The clock is on the wall. The TV is in front of the wall . . .)

Prepositions 3

A Match the vocabulary words with their meanings.

1 ___ lóutī		**a**	window
2 ___ zuǒbiān		**b**	stairs
3 ___ pángbiān		**c**	left, to the left of
4 ___ mén		**d**	door
5 ___ shūcài		**e**	in the middle of, between
6 ___ zhōngjiān		**f**	vegetables
7 ___ yòubiān		**g**	ball
8 ___ duìmiàn		**h**	next to, beside
9 ___ chuānghù		**i**	across from, opposite of; face to face
10 ___ qiú		**j**	right, to the right of

B Answer the questions using the words in parentheses.

Ex: Dàxué zài nǎ lǐ? (across from the park) → Dàxué zài gōngyuánde duìmiàn.

1 Diànyǐngyuàn zài nǎ lǐ? (next to the museum) _____

2 Túshūguǎn zài nǎ lǐ? (to the right of the art gallery) _____

3 Zhōngguó cāntīng zài nǎ lǐ? (across from the gas station) _____

4 Nǐ jiā zài nǎ lǐ? (next to Dàwèi's house) _____

5 Gāozhōng zài nǎ lǐ? (to the left of the amusement park) _____

6 Jiǔbā zài nǎ lǐ? (behind the convenience store) _____

C Match the following questions with the answers that make the most sense.

1 ___ Zhuōzi zài nǎ lǐ?		**a**	Zài bīngxiāngde lǐmiàn.
2 ___ Nǐde Yīngwén liànxíběn zài nǎ lǐ?		**b**	Zài yīyuànde pángbiān.
3 ___ Níngméngzhī zài nǎ lǐ?		**c**	Zài yǐzide zhōngjiān.
4 ___ Fàndiàn zài nǎ lǐ?		**d**	Zài shūbāode lǐmiàn.

D Given the answer, write the question.

Ex: A: Kāfēitīng zài wǒde bàngōngshìde yòubiān. → Q: Kāfēitīng zài nǎ lǐ?

1 A: Zài. Qiúchǎng zài hǎitānde qiánmiàn.

Q: _____

2 A: Bú zài. Xǐyīdiàn bú zài gāozhōngde duìmiàn.

Q: _____

3 A: Tāde xuéxiào zài Shànghǎi.

Q: _____

4 A: Jiānádà zài Měiguóde shàngmiàn.

Q: _____

5 A: Mòxīgē zài Měiguóde xiàmiàn.

Q: _____

6 A: Zài. Wǒde nǚpéngyǒu zài bàngōngshì.

Q: _____

E Your friend is visiting you from abroad, but you're out of the house when they first arrive. Leave a note for them, giving instructions about where to find places, like the bank, the school, the park, etc., or any useful items around the house.

Joey! I'm so glad you're in town for the week! Anyway, I know you don't really know your way around town yet, so here's some info about where some of my favorite places are located. If you get lost, don't worry. You'll find your way back to my garage eventually.

Ex: Diànyǐngyuàn zài gōngyuánde pángbiān.
Cāntīng zài diànyǐngyuànde yòubiān.
Wǒde dàxué zài bówùguǎnde duìmiàn.
Chāojí shìchǎng zài túshūguǎnde zuǒbiān.

_____

_____

_____

_____

_____

_____

Yào vs. Xiǎng 1

A Are the new vocabulary words matched correctly? If not, give the correct translation whenever you spot an error.

Ex: liǎn – face (Correct); tóufǎ – head (Incorrect: hair)

1 xǐ (zǎo) – to shave (beard) _____

2 shuā (yá) – to brush (teeth) _____

3 guā (húzi) – to wash (to take a shower) _____

4 shū (tóufa) – to cut / trim (hair) _____

5 zāng – dirty, filthy _____

6 jiǎn (tóufa) – to comb (hair) _____

B Use the words in parentheses to provide long answers to the following questions.

Ex: Bàba xiǎng qù nǎ lǐ? (his friend's house) → Bàba xiǎng qù tā(de) péngyǒude jiā.

1 Tā xiǎng qù nǎ lǐ? (the supermarket) _____

2 Míngtiān nǐ yào jiǎn tóufǎ ma? (yes) _____

3 Nǐmen xiǎng qù nǎ lǐ? (the zoo) _____

4 Nǐ yào mǎi nàběn shū ma? (yes) _____

5 Shéi yào hē yībēi guǒzhī? (my daughter) _____

6 Jīntiān tāmen xiǎng qù nǎ lǐ? (the beach) _____

C Given the answer, write the question.

1 **A:** Míngnián wǒ xiǎng qù Lúndūn.   **Q:** _____

2 **A:** Jīnnián tā yào qù Xīnjiāpō.   **Q:** _____

3 **A:** Wǒmen xiǎng qù Yìdàlì.   **Q:** _____

4 **A:** Míngtiān támen yào qù túshūguǎn.   **Q:** _____

5 **A:** Hòutiān wǒ érzi xiǎng qù xǐyīdiàn.   **Q:** _____

6 **A:** Jīntiān wǒ nǚ'ér yào qù xuéxiào.   **Q:** _____

D Use "xiǎng" to say what you would like to do and where you would like to go using the time expressions which are in bold.

Ex: Hòutiān wǒ xiǎng qù dǎ lánqiú. (The day after tomorrow I would like to go play basketball.)

1 **Jīntiān** wǒ xiǎng (qù) _____

_____

2 **Xīngqīsān** wǒ xiǎng (qù) _____

_____

3 **Míngtiān** wǒ xiǎng (qù) _____

_____

4 **Míngnián** wǒ xiǎng (qù) _____

_____

E Write a message to your friend inviting him / her to go out for the weekend. Where do you want to go? What do you want to do there? Don't forget to use time expressions in your sentences!

From: xxxxxxxxxxxx
Date: xxxxxxxxxx
To: Lily
Subject: Go out for the weekend

Lily, nǐ hǎo! I'm doing a lot of cool stuff this weekend, and if you'd like to join me, that would be great! If not, go find a new best friend! Anyway, here's what I'm thinking:

Ex: Xīngqīliù wǒ xiǎng qù cāntīng chīfàn. Wǒ yě xiǎng qù diànyǐngyuàn kàn diànyǐng. Wǒmen yě kěyǐ qù gōngyuán dǎ lánqiú. Xīngqītiān wǒ xiǎng qù hǎitān yóuyǒng. Nǐ xiǎng qù ma?

_____

_____

_____

_____

_____

Yào vs. Xiǎng 2

A **Match the new vocabulary words with their definitions.**

1 ___ chǎofàn
2 ___ fèn
3 ___ wǎn
4 ___ diǎn (cài)
5 ___ tái
6 ___ bù
7 ___ báifàn
8 ___ chūnjuǎn

a MW for vehicles, machines, electronic objects
b fried rice
c white rice
d to order (food)
e bowl; MW for bowls
f spring roll
g a portion, a share, an order of something
h MW for movies, films

B **Write long answers using the words in parentheses.**

1 Tā xiǎng diǎn shénme? (beef fried rice) _____

2 Nǐde fùqīn xiǎng hē shénme? (white wine) _____

3 Nǐmende mǔqīn xiǎng zuò shénme? (cook) _____

4 Lily xiǎng bù xiǎng hē yībēi lǜchá? (Yes) _____

5 Nàbù diànyǐng hǎokàn ma? (Yes) _____

6 Zhètái diànshì hěn guì ma? (No) _____

C **Given the answer, write the question.**

1 **A:** Xiǎng. Mìshū xiǎng zhǎo xīnde gōngzuò.   **Q:** _____

2 **A:** Bù xiǎng. Wǒ bù xiǎng qù hǎitān.   **Q:** _____

3 **A:** Yào. Wǒ yào mài nàtái diànnǎo.   **Q:** _____

4 **A:** Bú yào. Tāmen bú yào diǎn chūnjuǎn.   **Q:** _____

5 **A:** Xiǎng. Lǎoshī hěn xiǎng tāde nǚpéngyǒu.   **Q:** _____

D **Unscramble the sentences, then translate them into English.**

1 yào / chúshī / mǎi / dāozi / xīnde _____

2 wǒ / xiǎng / hěn / mǎi / chēzi / nàbù _____

3 bù / xǐhuān / zhètái / tā / diànshì _____

4 xiǎng / diǎn / wǒmen / sānwǎn / báifàn _____

E Translate the following using "yào" or "xiǎng" (or both) to complete the following sentences.

Ex: I would like to go to Russia next year. → Míngnián wǒ xiǎng qù Éguó.

1 She wants to order chicken fried rice. _____

2 He is going to go see the dentist tomorrow. _____

3 We have to brush our teeth. _____

4 I really miss my husband. _____

5 They would like to sell their house. _____

Yào vs. Xiǎng 3

 A **76.01 Fill in the blanks with the words you hear.**

Dàwèi:	_____ shì wǒde shēngrì.
Pèishān:	Nǐ jǐ suì?
Dàwèi:	Wǒ shí suì. Míngtiān shì wǒde shēngrì _____. Nǐ xiǎng lái ma?
Pèishān:	Xiǎng. Wǒ xiǎng qù nǐde shēngrì pàiduì, dànshì wǒ bù néng qù.
Dàwèi:	_____?
Pèishān:	Yīnwèi míngtiān wǒ yào qù _____.
Dàwèi:	Wǒ hěn xǐhuān Luòshānjī yě xǐhuān _____.
Pèishān:	Wǒ yě shì. _____ zhēnde hěn piàoliàng.

B **Are the translations correct? Rewrite the incorrect sentences correctly.**

1 Xīngqīwǔ wǒmen xiǎng chūqù. (We would like to go out on Friday.)

_____

2 Nǐ kě bù kěyǐ qù Dàwèide pàiduì? (Can Dàwèi go to the party?)

_____

3 Bàbamāma fēicháng xǐhuān Luòshānjīde tiānqì. (Mom and Dad really like the weather in Los Angeles.)

_____

4 Shéi yào mài nàbù lǜsède chēzi? (Who wants to sell that green car?)

_____

5 Zhèwǎn tāng rè bú rè? (Is that bowl of soup hot?)

_____

6 Nàbù hēisède chēzi tài guì! (This black car is too expensive!)

_____

7 Zhètái dà(de) diànshì hǎo piányí! (This big television is so cheap!)

_____

C Unscramble the sentences.

1 diànnǎo / bǐjìběn / hěn / hǎoyòng / nàtái _____

2 zhèbù / diànyǐng / tài / bú / hǎokàn _____

3 chūnjuǎn / nàxiē / guì / zhēn _____

4 xiǎo / zhèxiē / tài / bēizi _____

5 báifàn / bù / zhèwǎn / hǎochī _____

6 nàgè / chāo / dàxuéshēng / cōngmíng _____

D What are you going to do next year? What would you like to do next year? Write three sentences for each.

Ex: Míngnián wǒ yào qù kàn yáyī. / Míngnián wǒ xiǎng zhǎo (yīfèn) gōngzuò.

You are going to:

1 _____

2 _____

3 _____

You would like to:

1 _____

2 _____

3 _____

Yǒu 2

A Match the words and definitions.

1 ___ shūjià   a there is / are

2 ___ shūguì   b how much, how many (smaller numbers up to 15 or 20)

3 ___ bānjí   c how much, how many (for money and larger numbers)

4 ___ yǒu   d a class

5 ___ duōshǎo   e a province (part of a country)

6 ___ jǐ   f bookshelf

7 ___ shěng   g bookcase

B Now take it a step further. Match the Chinese and English translations.

1 ___ Shùshàng yǒu jǐzhī niǎo?   a How many animals are there in the zoo?

2 ___ Shùshàng yǒu sānzhī niǎo.   b There are three birds in the tree.

3 ___ Dòngwùyuánde lǐmiàn yǒu duōshǎo dòngwù?   c How many birds are there in the tree?

4 ___ Dòngwùyuánde lǐmiàn yǒu 150 zhī dòngwù.   d There are 150 animals in the zoo.

C Remember that you can drop "de" and "-miàn". Convert the prepositional phrases to their shorter forms.

Ex: Bīngxiāngde lǐmiàn yǒu hěn duō dàn. → Bīngxiāng lǐ yǒu hěn duō dàn.

1 Zhuōzide shàngmiàn yǒu liǎngtái bǐjìběn diànnǎo. _____

2 Nǐde chēzide lǐmiàn yǒu hěn duō lèsè. _____

3 Yǐzide xiàmiàn yǒu yīzhī qiānbǐ. _____

4 Kǎoxiāngde lǐmiàn yǒu méi yǒu miànbāo? _____

5 Dìtǎnde shàngmiàn yǒu liǎngzhī māo. _____

6 Wēibōlúde lǐmiàn yǒu yīwǎn báifàn. _____

D Would you use "jǐ" or "duōshǎo" to ask about the following?

Ex: six people → jǐ

1. _____ the population of your town
2. _____ the number of pets your best friend has
3. _____ the number of students at your university
4. _____ the number of bananas in your refrigerator
5. _____ the number of countries in the world
6. _____ the number of people who live in your house

E Translate the following questions with "jǐ" or "duōshǎo" and then answer the questions using the numbers in parentheses.

1. Nǐde péngyǒu jiā yǒu jǐzhī gǒu? (2) _____
2. Jiùjīnshān yǒu duōshǎo rén? (900,000) _____
3. Tāmen jiā yǒu jǐtái diànshì? (3) _____
4. Nǐmende xiǎohái yǒu duōshǎo làbǐ? (64) _____

F Read the short conversation in which Pèishān and Dàwèi describe their hometowns and answer the questions.

Pèishān:	Nǐ jiā zài nǎ lǐ?
Dàwèi:	Wǒ jiā zài Zhījiāgē. Zhījiāgē shì (yīgè) hěn yǒuqùde chéngshì. Zhījiāgē yǒu hěn duō bówùguǎn, yě yǒu hěn duō hěn piàoliàngde gōngyuán. Nǐ ne? Nǐ jiā zài nǎ lǐ?
Pèishān:	Wǒ jiā zài Luòshānjī. Luòshānjīde tiānqì hěn wēnnuǎn. Luòshānjī yǒu hěn duō hǎitān. Luòshānjī yě yǒu hěn duō hěn yǒumíngde yǎnyuán.

1. Where does Dàwèi live?
2. Where does Pèishān live?
3. How is the weather in Pèishān's home town?
4. List two cool features about Dàwèi's home town.
5. Besides the weather, what else does Pèishān mention about her home town?

Present Progressive Tense

A Translate the following present progressive English sentences into Chinese.

1 He is running. _____

2 She is dancing. _____

3 Amy is jumping. _____

4 I am eating breakfast. _____

5 They are playing soccer. _____

6 We are speaking Chinese. _____

B **78.01 Listen and write down what the people are doing now.**

1 Nàxiē lǜshī zài _____.

2 Wǒ zài _____.

3 Zhège lǎoshī zài _____.

4 Lily zài _____.

5 Tā zài _____.

6 Tāmen zài _____.

C Choose the correct verb to complete the following sentences.

1 Tāmen zài **xuéxí / chī** Fǎwén. _____

2 Māma zài **dǎ / xǐ** májiàng. _____

3 Wǒde péngyǒu zài **tīng / kàn** yīnyuè. _____

4 Nǐmende wàipó zài **hē / zuò** fàn. _____

5 Tāde wàigōng zài **tán / dǎ** jítā. _____

D Unscramble these sentences.

1 hùshì / zài / nàgè / yīshēng / bāng _____

2 zhège / zài / jūnrén / pǎobù _____

3 yǎnyuán / nàgè / chī / wǎncān / zài _____

4 zài / shéi / kāi / chē / wǒde / ? _____

E Indicate whether "zài" is being used as a preposition or to help form the present progressive tense.

1 Lín Xiānshēng zài qiúchǎng ma? _____

2 Lín Tàitai zài pàochá ma? _____

3 Nǐ zài bú zài jiā? _____

4 Nàgè nánrén zài qí shéide mótuōchē? _____

5 Tāde fùmǔ zài yóuyǒng. _____

F Leave a voicemail message for a friend, letting him / her know where you are, what you are doing and where you are going to be in the next hour (so you can meet up).

Ex: Yo, Barack!

Xiànzài wǒ zài cāntīng. Wǒ zài chī wǎncān. Wǒ yě zài kàn wǒde Zhōngwén kèběn. Nǐ ne? Nǐ zài nǎ lǐ? Nǐ zhèng zài zuò shénme? Nǐ xiǎng bù xiǎng lái cāntīng zhǎo wǒ?

More Present Progressive Tense

A Select the word which best fits each sentence. Then say the whole sentence out loud, paying close attention to pronunciation and tone.

1 Nàgè xuéshēng zài **fùxí / gōngzuò** tāde zuòyè.

2 Bàba zhèng zài kàn **xīnwén / gōngzuò**.

3 Wǒ **zuò / zài** chī wǔcān.

4 Xiànzài wǒ hěn máng. Wǒ zài **gōngzuò / gōngxǐ**.

B 79.01 What are Dàwèi and Pèishān's family members doing right now? Listen to the statements and fill in the blanks with the words you hear.

1 Dàwèide bàba zhèng zài _____.

2 Pèishānde mèimei zhèng zài _____.

3 Dàwèide gēge zhèng zài _____.

4 Pèishānde dìdi zhèng zài _____.

5 Dàwèide māma zhèng zài _____.

6 Pèishānde jiějie zhèng zài _____.

C Find and fix the errors in the following translations.

Nǐ zhèng zài zuò shénme?	*What are you doing?*	
Ex: Tā zhèng zài wán yóuxì.	He is (washing dishes).	_playing a game_____
1 Wǒ zhèng zài fùxí Zhōngwén.	I am speaking Chinese.	_____
2 Tāde gōngzuò zài Niǔyuē.	He is working in New York.	_____
3 Shéi zài chànggē?	Where are you singing?	_____
4 Nǐ zài chī shénme?	What are you eating?	_____
5 Tāmen zài hē lǜchá ma?	They are drinking green tea.	_____
6 Wǒ tàitai zài cāntīng.	My wife is eating dinner.	_____

D **Indicate whether "zài" is being used as a preposition or to help form the present progressive tense.**

1 Lǎoshī zài jiāoshū. _____

2 Wǒde yīshēng zài yīyuàn. _____

3 Lily zài tāde fángjiān. _____

4 Mángguǒ zài bīngxiāng lǐ ma? _____

5 Tāmen zài dǎ lánqiú. _____

Yes / No Questions Review

A Match the new vocabulary words to their meanings.

1 ___ fángdōng   **a** to rent

2 ___ zū   **b** to pay money

3 ___ fùqián   **c** an apartment building, a block of flats

4 ___ zhuànqián   **d** a landlord

5 ___ gōngyù   **e** to earn money

B Make a To-do list for the day. What do you have to do? Where do you have to go?

> **To-do list**
>
> **Ex:** Jīntiān wǒ fēicháng máng. Wǒ yào qù fù (wǒde) fángdōng qián. Wǒ yě yào qù jiǎn tóufǎ. Yīnwèi wǒ hěn qióng, suǒyǐ wǒ yào qù zhǎo xīnde gōngzuò.
>
> _____
>
> _____
>
> _____
>
> _____
>
> _____

C Are the following short answers correct? Write out the correct sentence if there are any errors.

Ex: Nǐ yǒu méi yǒu píngbǎn diànnǎo? Yǒu. (Correct)

Nǐde bǐjìběn shì hēisède ma? Bù. (Incorrect) (Bú shì.)

1 Tāmen yào bú yào fùqián? Bú yào. _____

2 Nǐmen xiǎng bù xiǎng zū zhègè fángzi? Shì. _____

3 Bàba zài jiāyóuzhàn ma? Zài. _____

4 Tā huì dǎ bàngqiú ma? Bú huì. _____

5 Nǐde nánpéngyǒu gāo bù gāo? Shì. _____

6 Nǐde fángdōng xǐ bù xǐhuān nǐ? Xǐhuān. _____

D Translate the following sentences.

Ex: Shéi zài jiǎng diànhuà? → Who is talking on the phone?

1   Wèishénme nǐ bù xiǎng qù pàiduì? _____

2   Wo zài zhǎo gōngzuò. Wǒ xiǎng zhuān hěn duō qián. _____

3   Wǒ kě bù kěyǐ yòng nǐde gōngjù? _____

4   Tāmen yǒu méi yǒu chǒngwù? _____

5   Nǐmen xǐhuān xǐ wǎn ma? _____

6   Nàbēi hóngchá tàng bú tàng? _____

E Answer the following questions with long answers.

Ex: Tā zài zuò shénme? (reading his Chinese textbook) → Tā zài kàn tāde Zhōngwén kèběn.

1   Hùshì zài bú zài yīyuàn? (Yes) _____

2   Lǎobǎn zài bàngōngshì ma? (No) _____

3   Nǐmen xiǎng zū gōngyù ma? (Yes) _____

4   Lily yào hē píjiǔ háishì pútáojiǔ? (wine) _____

5   Pàiduì yǒu jǐgè rén? (16) _____

6   Nǐde jiārén xǐhuān qù qiúchǎng ma? (No) _____

Subject + Time + Action 1

A Complete the "cí" by adding the correct word part from the choices:

táng	diàn	guó	jú	fáng

1 yè_____   nightclub

2 chū_____   to leave the country; go abroad

3 yóu_____   post office

4 jiào_____   church

5 yào_____   pharmacy

6 miànbāo_____   bakery

B Translate the following from Chinese to English.

Ex: Xīngqīrì nǐ xiǎng qù jiàotáng ma? → Would you like to go to church on Sunday?

1 Dàhòutiān wǒmen yào qù miànbāodiàn. _____

2 Nǐ xīngqīliù xiǎng bù xiǎng qù yèdiàn? _____

3 Tāmen jīntiān zài jiā ma? _____

4 Nǐmen xiànzài zài chī zǎocān ma? _____

5 Liùyuè nǐ bàba yào chūguó ma? _____

6 Nǐ lǎopó zuótiān hěn lèi ma? _____

C Use the words in parentheses to provide long answers to the questions.

Ex: Nǐ qiántiān zài nǎ lǐ? (the post office) → Wǒ qiántiān zài yóujú.

1 Yàofáng zài nǎ lǐ? (across from the church) _____

2 Nǐmen xīngqīyī xiǎng qù nǎ lǐ? (the coffee shop) _____

3 Xiànzài Wáng Xiānshēng zài yàofáng ma? (No) _____

4 Xīngqīwǔ nǐ xiǎng qù yèdiàn ma? (Yes) _____

5 Tā jīntiān zài nǎ lǐ? (at the university) _____

6 Nǐde nǎinai zuótiān zài nǎ lǐ? (at the bakery) _____

D Choose the word that fits best with the rest of the sentence, then translate it into English.

Ex: Yīnwèi wǒ zuótiān hěn lèi, suǒyǐ wǒ bù xiǎng **shuìjiào** / (**chūqù**).

1 Yīnwèi jīntiān tāmen hěn wúliáo, suǒyǐ tāmen xiǎng qù **yīyuàn / yèdiàn**.

_____

2 Yīnwèi lǎoshī xiànzài zài Zhōngguó, suǒyǐ tā hěn **xiǎng / yào** tāde jiārén.

_____

3 Yīnwèi tā bù shūfú, suǒyǐ tā yào qù **yàofáng / yóujú**.

_____

4 Yīnwèi xiànzài shì bāyuè, suǒyǐ dàjiā xiǎng **miàobāodiàn / chūguó**.

_____

E Read the following conversation and answer the questions.

Dàwèi:	Pèishān, zǎoshàng hǎo! Nǐ jīntiān xiǎng bù xiǎng chūqù?
Pèishān:	Wǒ jīntiān bù néng chūqù. Wǒ yào zuò zuòyè.
Dàwèi:	Hǎo. Míngtiān ne? Nǐ míngtiān xiǎng qù bówùguǎn ma?
Pèishān:	Bù xiǎng. Bówùguǎn hěn wúliáo.
Dàwèi:	Hòutiān ne? Nǐ xiǎng bù xiǎng qù měishùguǎn?
Pèishān:	Bù xiǎng. Měishùguǎn yě hěn wúliáo.
Dàwèi:	Dàhòutiān ne? Nǐ dàhòutiān xiǎng lái wǒ jiā chī wǎncān ma?
Pèishān:	Xiǎng. Dàhòutiān wǒ xiǎng qù nǐ jiā chī wǎncān. Nǐ huì zhǔfàn ma?
Dàwèi:	Bú huì. Wǒ bú huì zhǔfàn, dànshì wǒ māma hěn huì. Nǐ xǐhuān chī shénme?
Pèishān:	Wǒ xǐhuān chī miàn.
Dàwèi:	Hǎo. Dàhòutiān jiàn.

1 Why can't Pèishān go out today?

_____

2 Does Pèishān want to go to the museum tomorrow? Why or why not?

_____

3 Where would Dàwèi like to go the day after tomorrow?

_____

4 What does Pèishān agree to do the day after the day after tomorrow?

_____

5 What does Pèishān like to eat?

_____

Subject + Time + Action 2

A Label the following vocabulary words as nouns (N) or verbs (V).

1 tuī _____

2 lǎba _____

3 dǎ _____

4 xiǎotíqín _____

5 bānjiā _____

6 gǔ _____

7 tán _____

8 lā _____

9 yínháng _____

10 chuī _____

11 kǒuqín _____

B Unscramble the following sentences.

Ex: nǐ / xǐhuān / wèishénme / gāngqín / tán? → Wèishénme nǐ xǐhuān tán gāngqín?
OR Nǐ wèishénme xǐhuān tán gāngqín?

1 jīntiān / yào / nǐ / liànxí / ma / xiǎotíqín / ? _____

2 huì / dǎ / shéi / gǔ / ? _____

3 xǐ / Lily / bù / chuī / xǐhuān / lǎba / ? _____

4 hěn / kǒuqín / piányí _____

C Answer the yes / no questions using the words in parentheses.

Ex: Tāmen huì bú huì tán jítā? (Yes) → Huì. Tāmen huì tán jítā.

1 Mike Lǎoshī huì dǎ gǔ ma? (Yes) _____

2 Nǐ xiǎng bù xiǎng kàn wǒde xiǎotíqín? (No) _____

3 Tā yào mǎi xīnde lǎba ma? (No) _____

4 Nǐmende péngyǒude gāngqín hěn guì ma? (Yes) _____

D 82.01 Which instruments can Dàwèi's family members play?

1 Dàwèide māma huì _____.

2 Dàwèide bàba yě huì _____.

3 Dàwèide gēge huì _____.

4 Dàwèide jiějie huì _____.

5 Dàwèide mèimei _____.

6 Dàwèide dìdi huì _____.

E Go around and ask your classmates or friends what instruments they can play and would like to learn how to play.

Ex:

1 John, nǐ huì tán jítā ma? Huì. Wǒ huì tán jítā. Nǐ huì dǎ gǔ ma? Bú huì. Wǒ bú huì dǎ gǔ. Nǐ xiǎng xué dǎ gǔ ma? Xiǎng. Wǒ xiǎng xué dǎ gǔ.

2 Samantha, Nǐ huì bú huì tán gāngqín? Huì. Wǒ huì tán gāngqín. Wǒ yě huì lā xiǎotíqín. Nǐ xiǎng bù xiǎng xué chuī lǎba? Bù xiǎng. Wǒ bù xiǎng xué chuī lǎba.

Subject + Time + Action 3

A **Match the vocabulary words with their definitions.**

1 ___ jiàrì   **a** to leave the house; (lit. to go out the door)

2 ___ zhōumò   **b** to release; to let out; set off

3 ___ hánjià   **c** to have a vacation / holiday

4 ___ jiérì   **d** summer vacation

5 ___ fàngjià   **e** winter vacation

6 ___ chūmén   **f** a day off; a non-working day

7 ___ shǔjià   **g** holiday; a festival (e.g. Christmas; New Year's Day)

8 ___ fàng   **h** the weekend

B **Answer the following questions using the words in parentheses.**

Ex: Nǐ jiàrì xǐhuān zuò shénme? (play tennis) → Wǒ jiàrì xǐhuān dǎ wǎngqiú.

1 Nàgè xuéshēng jǐyuè fàngjià? (July) _____

2 Zhègè jiàoshòu jǐyuè fàng shǔjià? (May) _____

3 Zhèxiē gāozhōngshēng xīngqījǐ fàng hánjià? (Friday) _____

4 Míngtiān shì bú shì jiérì? (Yes) _____

5 Nǐde bàbamāma jǐdiàn xiǎng chūmén? (5:30) _____

C **Look at the answers, then fill in the blanks with the correct question words.**

Ex: Tāmen ___xīngqījǐ___ yào bānjiā? Tāmen xīngqīsì yào bānjiā.

1 Huáng Xiānshēng _____ yào chūmén?

    Huáng Xiānshēng sìdiǎn èrshí fēn yào chūmén.

2 Chén Tàitai _____ xiǎng chūguó?

    Chén Tàitai jiǔyuè xiǎng chūguó.

3 Nàxiē dàxuéshēng _____ xiǎng dǎ pīngpāngqiú?

    Nàxiē dàxuéshēng qīdiǎn bàn xiǎng dǎ pīngpāngqiú.

4 Nǐ _____ fàng shǔjià?

    Wǒ wǔyuè èrshíwǔ hào fàng shǔjià.

5 Nǐmen _____ yào qù yóujú?

    Wǒmen xīngqī'èr yào qù yóujú.

6 Pèishān _____ yào qù shēngrì pàiduì?

    Pèishān sānyuè sānshí hào yào qù shēngrì pàiduì.

D Translate the following sentences.

Ex: Wǒde nǚpéngyǒu zhōumò xǐhuān qù kàn diànyǐng. →
My girlfriend likes to go see movies on the weekend.

1 Nǐ bàba jǐdiǎn yào chūmén? _____

2 Lily jǐyuè fàng hánjià? _____

3 Tā xǐhuān shénme jiérì? _____

4 Tāmen xǐhuān fàng shǔjià ma? _____

E What season do you like? Write a brief paragraph about why you like a certain season of the year.

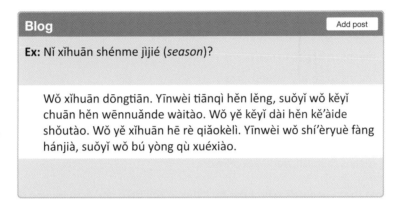

Blog   Add post

Ex: Nǐ xǐhuān shénme jìjié (*season*)?

Wǒ xǐhuān dōngtiān. Yīnwèi tiānqì hěn lěng, suǒyǐ wǒ kěyǐ chuān hěn wēnnuǎnde wàitào. Wǒ yě kěyǐ dài hěn kě'àide shǒutào. Wǒ yě xǐhuān hē rè qiǎokèlì. Yīnwèi wǒ shí'èryuè fàng hánjià, suǒyǐ wǒ bú yòng qù xuéxiào.

Blog   Add post

Nǐ xǐhuān shénme jìjié (season)? _____

_____

_____

_____

_____

_____

_____

Subject + Time + Action 4

A Fill in the blanks with the correct vocabulary words from the word bank.

kè	táng	shàngkè	shàngbān	xiàkè	xiàbān	kāishǐ

1 _____ means class; course; lesson

2 _____ means to begin; to start

3 _____ means to go to / attend class

4 _____ means to finish class / school

5 _____ means to go to / start work / be at work

6 _____ is the MW for classes; lessons

7 _____ means to finish work; get off work

B 84.01 Complete these people's schedules by filling in the time and activity you hear.

1 Bàba _____ _____.

2 Māma _____ kāishǐ _____.

3 Lisa _____ yào _____.

4 Tom _____ _____.

5 Nàgè shāngrén _____ _____.

C Given the answer, write the question.

Ex: **A:** Wǒ érzi bādiǎn bàn shàngkè. → **Q:** Nǐ érzi jǐdiǎn shàngkè?

1 **A:** Nàgè nǚrén bādiǎn kāishǐ shàngbān. **Q:** _____

2 **A:** Zhègè jiàoliàn xīngqīsān xiǎng liànxí tī zúqiú. **Q:** _____

3 **A:** Wǒmende jiàoshòu sìdiǎn xiàkè. **Q:** _____

4 **A:** Lily èryuè yào qù Ài'ěrlán. **Q:** _____

5 **A:** Nàxiē jǐngchá shídiǎn xiàbān. **Q:** _____

D Are the following translations correct? Fix the mistakes if there are any.

Ex: Wǒ jīntiān yǒu liǎngtáng kè. I have two classes today. (Correct)

Zuótiān tā yǒu sāntáng kè. He / She had five classes yesterday.
(Incorrect. He / She had three classes yesterday.)

1 Míngtiān lǎoshì yǒu méi yǒu kè? (Does the teacher have class tomorrow?)

_____

2 Nǐmen hòutiān yào bú yào shàngbān? (Do you guys have to go to school the day after tomorrow?)

_____

3 Dàhòutiān wǒmen yào shàngke yě yào shàngbān. (In three days, we have to go to school and go to work.)

_____

4 Dàwèi xīngqīliù fàngjià. (Dàwèi has a day off on Sunday.)

_____

E Look at the five-day schedule and fill in one activity for each. An example has been given.

Five-day schedule

Monday	Tuesday	Wednesday	Thursday	Friday
Wǒ xīngqīyī wán diàndòng yóuxì (I play video games on Monday.)				

Subject + Time + Action 5

A **Match the courses with their English translations.**

1	____ diànnǎo kè		**a**	English class
2	____ lìshǐ kè		**b**	computer class
3	____ tǐyù kè		**c**	Chinese class
4	____ Yīngwén kè		**d**	history class
5	____ Zhōngwén kè		**e**	physical education class

B **Give the correct translation if you spot any errors in the following ordinal numbers.**

Ex: dìliù – sixth (Correct); dìshíyī – twenty-first (Incorrect – eleventh)

1 dìshí'èr – twelfth _____

5 dìwǔ – fifth _____

2 dìsānshí – thirteenth _____

6 dìqī – third _____

3 dìbā – eighth _____

7 dì jiǔ – second _____

4 dìshí – first _____

8 dìsì – tenth _____

Now translate the following ordinal numbers into Chinese.

9 23rd _____

12 50th _____

10 17th _____

13 84th _____

11 2nd _____

14 14th _____

C **Unscramble the following sentences.**

Ex: jǐdiǎn / tāmen / xiàkè / ? → Tāmen jǐdiǎn xiàkè?

1 nǐmen / yǒu / jīntiān / kè / jǐtáng / ? _____

2 jīntiān / Lily / yǒu / wǔtáng / kè _____

3 tǐyù / jǐdiǎn / shàng / nǐ / kè / ? _____

4 nǚ'ér / wǒ / míngtiān / kè / Yīngwén / yǒu _____

D **Use the words in parentheses to write long answers to the following questions. Then translate the answers into English.**

Ex: Nǐ jīntiān yào shàng Yīngwén kè ma? (Yes) Yào. Wǒ jīntiān yào shàng Yīngwén kè. (Yes, I have to attend English class today.)

1 Tāmende Zhōngwén kè nán bù nán? (Not difficult) _____

2 Nàgè jiàoshòu míngtiān yào shàng jǐtáng kè? (2) _____

3 Nǐmen xīngqījǐ shàng shùxué kè? (Tuesday) _____

4 Nǐde háizi jǐdiǎn xiàkè? (3 o'clock) _____

5 Tā xǐ bù xǐhuān tāde diànnǎo kè? (Yes) _____

E Given the answer, write the question.

Ex: **A:** Shì. Wǒde péngyǒude shùxué kè hěn jiǎndān. →
   Q: Nǐde péngyǒude shùxué kè hěn jiǎndān ma?

1 **A:** Xiǎng. Wǒmen xiǎng kāishǐ xué Xībānyáwén. **Q:** _____

2 **A:** Robert xīngqīsì shàng diànnǎo kè. **Q:** _____

3 **A:** Wǒ shídiǎn shàng shùxué kè. **Q:** _____

4 **A:** Yǒu. Zuótiān tā yǒu sìtáng kè. **Q:** _____

5 **A:** Nàxiē gāozhōngshēng sāndiǎn bàn xiàkè. **Q:** _____

6 **A:** Wǒde xiānshēng wǔdiǎn xiàbān. **Q:** _____

F Dàwèi and Pèishān would like to see a movie this week, but they have conflicting schedules. Help them find a movie that they both can attend.

Art Movie Theater Schedule

MONDAY	TUESDAY	WEDNESDAY
1 p.m. – Movie 1 5 p.m. – Movie 3	3 p.m. – Movie 2	1 p.m. – Movie 1 5 p.m. – Movie 3

Dàwèi:	Wǒ hěn xiǎng qù kàn yībù xīnde diànyǐng.
Pèishān:	Wǒ yě hěn xiǎng qù!
Dàwèi:	Nǐ xīngqīyī yào shàngkè ma?
Pèishān:	Yào. Wǒ shí'èr diǎn kāishǐ shàngkè. Wǒ wǔdiǎn xiàkè.
Dàwèi:	Xīngqī'èr ne? Nǐ xīngqī'èr yǒu kè ma?
Pèishān:	Yǒu. Wǒ xīngqī'èr yě yǒu kè. Nǐ ne?
Dàwèi:	Méi yǒu. Wǒ méi yǒu kè dànshì wǒ yào shàngbān.
Pèishān:	Nǐ jǐdiǎn xiàbān?
Dàwèi:	Wǒ wǔ diǎn bàn xiàbān
Pèishān:	Nǐ xīngqīsān yǒu jǐtáng kè?
Dàwèi:	Wǒ xīngqīsān yǒu liǎngtáng kè. Wǒ sān diǎn xiàkè. Nǐ ne?
Pèishān:	Xīngqīsān wǒ méi yǒu kè.
Dàwèi:	Nǐ yǒu gōngzuò ma?
Pèishān:	Méi yǒu. Wǒ méi yǒu gōngzuò.

The movie that they will be going to see is: _____

What day and time will they see it? _____

Shénme Shíhòu

A Match the vocabulary words to their definitions.

1 _____ jiéhūn   a a classical music concert

2 _____ yǎnzòuhuì   b to marry; to get married

3 _____ gējù   c (western) opera

4 _____ huí   d a concert

5 _____ yǎnchànghuì   e to graduate

6 _____ bìyè   f to return; to go back

B 86.01 Fill in the blanks with the words you hear.

1 Dàwèi shénme shíhòu yào _____?

2 Pèishān shénme shíhòu yào _____ _____?

3 Dàwèi míngnián xiǎng qù _____ _____.

4 Pèishān zuótiān zài _____.

5 Dàwèi hòunián xiǎng _____.

6 Pèishān shénme shíhòu yào _____ Jiānádà?

C Translate the following from Chinese to English.

Ex: Tāmen míngnián xiǎng jiéhūn ma? → Would they like to get married next year?

1 Nǐ shénme shíhòu kāishǐ shàngbān? _____

2 Lily shénme shíhòu yào fàngjià? _____

3 Hòutiān shì bú shì xīngqīrì? _____

4 Nǐ érzi shénme shíhòu yào qù kàn yǎnchànghuì? _____

5 Yīnwèi tā jīnnián yào bìyè, suǒyǐ tā hěn gāoxìng. _____

D Write sentences about when you or people you know are going to do the following:

Ex: graduate → Wǒde nǚpéngyǒu míngnián yào bìyè.

1 go see a concert _____

2 attend class _____

3 get out of class _____

4 get married _____

5 return to England _____

E Finish the e-mail to your friend in China, explaining that you have a hectic schedule for the rest of the year and will not be able to go see her. (Oh, and certainly you'll want to use some of your new vocabulary!)

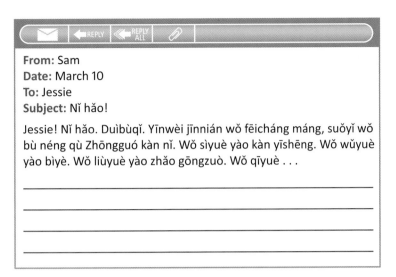

From: Sam
Date: March 10
To: Jessie
Subject: Nǐ hǎo!

Jessie! Nǐ hǎo. Duìbùqǐ. Yīnwèi jīnnián wǒ fēicháng máng, suǒyǐ wǒ bù néng qù Zhōngguó kàn nǐ. Wǒ sìyuè yào kàn yīshēng. Wǒ wǔyuè yào bìyè. Wǒ liùyuè yào zhǎo gōngzuò. Wǒ qīyuè . . .

_____

_____

_____

_____

Sequencing Periods of Time 1

A **Are the following translations correct? Correct the ones that contain errors.**

Ex: jīnnián qiūtiān (this fall) (Correct); jīnnián dōngtiān (this spring) (Incorrect) (this winter)

1 míngtiān wǎnshàng (tomorrow evening) _____

2 zuótiān zǎoshàng (yesterday afternoon) _____

3 jīnnián yīyuè (this January) _____

4 qùnián xiàtiān (last summer) _____

5 xīngqīwǔ wǎnshàng (Friday morning) _____

6 xīngqīrì zǎoshàng (Sunday afternoon) _____

7 2013 nián xiàtiān (the summer of 2013) _____

8 2015 nián jiǔyuè (August of 2015) _____

B **Unscramble the following sentences.**

Ex: xīngqīyī / wǒmen / zǎoshàng / qù / yào / kāfēitīng →
Wǒmen xīngqīyī zǎoshàng yào qù kāfēitīng.

1 xiǎng / hòutiān / wǎnshàng / Lily / Měiguó / huí _____

2 tā / érzi / qīdiǎn / zǎoshàng / zǎocān / chī _____

3 wǒ / wǎnshàng / liùdiǎn bàn / nǚ'ér/ chūfā / xiǎng _____

4 yào / jīnnián / bāyuè / tāmen / chūguó _____

C **Given the answer, write the question.**

Ex: A: Lèi. Tā zuótiān wǎnshàng hěn lèi. → **Q:** Tā zuótiān wǎnshàng lèi bú lèi?

1 **A:** Bù máng. Wǒ qiántiān xiàwǔ bù máng.

Q: _____

2 **A:** Wǒ bàbamāma míngtiān wǎnshàng xiǎng huíjiā.

Q: _____

3 **A:** Yào. Dàwèi jīntiān wǎnshàng yào qù cāntīng chīfàn.

Q: _____

4 **A:** Xiǎng. Wǒ jiějie xīngqīsì wǎnshàng xiǎng zhǔ miàn.

Q: _____

1 Nǐde péngyǒu _____ yào qù jiàotáng.

2 Mike Lǎoshī _____ xiǎng dǎ gǎnlǎnqiú.

3 Wǒmen _____ yào qù yèdiàn.

4 Nàgè dàxuéshēng _____ qù shuìjiào.

5 Zhègè háizi _____ méi yǒu zuòyè.

6 Wǒ _____ yào qù Bāxī.

Sequencing Periods of Time 2

A Use the words in the word bank to fill in the blanks for the following vocabulary words.

fēi	chē	jī

1 ____jī   – an airplane
2 huǒ____   – a train
3 gōnggòng qì____ – a bus
4 ____piào   – a bus / train ticket
5 ____piào   – plane ticket

B Give long answers using the words in parentheses.

Ex: Nǐde tàitai jǐdiǎn jǐfēn yào xià fēijī? (2:10) → Wǒde tàitai 2 diǎn 10 fēn yào xià fēijī.

1 Huǒchēzhàn zài nǎ lǐ? (next to the bank)

_____

2 Suzy yǒu méi yǒu jīpiào? (No)

_____

3 **Q:** Nǐ zài zuò shénme? (waiting for the bus)

_____

4 Tā xīngqījǐ xiǎng zuò huǒchē qù Niǔyuē? (Monday)

_____

5 Tāmen shénme shíhòu yào shàng gōngchē? (this afternoon)

_____

6 Wú Xiānshēng xiǎng mǎi jǐzhāng chēpiào? (5)

_____

C Given the answer, write the question.

Ex: A: Wǒde jiārén jīntiān wǎnshàng liùdiǎn yào xià huǒchē.
    Q: Nǐde jiārén shénme shíhòu yào xià huǒchē?

1 A: Wǒmen míngtiān xiàwǔ sāndiǎn yào chūfā.

    Q: _____

2 A: Tāmen xīngqīsì zǎoshàng xiǎng huí jiā.

    Q: _____

3 A: Tāmende wàigōng jīnnián xiàtiān xiǎng bānjiā.

    Q: _____

4 A: Lily shíyuè èrshíhào yào zuò fēijī qù Rìběn.

    Q: _____

5 A: Nǐde chēpiào zài zhuōzi shàng.

    Q: _____

D Unscramble the sentences.

Ex: jīpiào / bú / zhèzhāng / guì → Zhèzhāng jīpiào bú guì.

1 nàzhāng / shì / chēpiào / shéide / ? _____

2 dà / bú / huǒchēzhàn / dà / ? _____

3 zài / nǎ lǐ / jīchǎng / ? _____

4 bāshì / nàtái / hěn / kuài _____

5 jǐdiǎn / nǐmen / huǒchē / shàng / ? _____

E Answer the following questions in Chinese using the timetable.

Departures	Arrivals
Flight 835 – Los Angeles 5:25 p.m.	Flight 140 – New York 8:00 p.m.
Flight 231 – Beijing 6:12 a.m.	Flight 900 – Tokyo 10:30 p.m.
Flight 378 – London 1:45 p.m.	Flight 619 – Shanghai 5:15 a.m.

1 Bob yào qù Lúndūn. Tā jǐdiǎn zuò fēijī? _____

2 Sarah zài Flight 619. Tā jǐdiǎn xià fēijī? _____

3 Jim yào qù Běijīng. Tā jǐdiǎn zuò fēijī? _____

4 Kim zài Flight 140. Tā jǐdiǎn xià fēijī? _____

Gè For New Time Words

A Match the time phrases with their definitions.

1 ___ yuèlì   a last month

2 ___ zhègèxīngqī   b last week

3 ___ xiàgèyuè   c this month

4 ___ xiàgèxīngqī   d next week

5 ___ zhègèyuè   e next month

6 ___ shànggèxīngqī   f this week

7 ___ shànggèyuè   g monthly calendar

B 89.01 Fill in the time Lily was at or will be going to the following places.

1 Lily _____ yào qù Bōlán.

2 Lily _____ xiǎng qù Jiāzhōu.

3 Lily _____ yào qù jīchǎng.

4 Lily _____ zài Luòshānjī.

5 Lily _____ yào zuò fēijī qù Ōuzhōu.

6 Lily _____ zài Àozhōu.

C Are the translations correct? Correct the errors if there are any.

Ex: Wǒ zhègèyuè hěn máng. (I am very busy this month.) → Correct

Wǒ shànggèyuè hěn nánguò. (I was very excited last month.) → Incorrect –
I was very sad last month.

1 Nàgè nánrén xiàgèxīngqīwǔ yào qù yīyuàn. (That man is going to go to the hospital next Friday.)

_____

2 Zhègè nǚrén shànggèxīngqīrì zài jiàotáng. (This woman was at the post office last Saturday.)

_____

3 Tāmen xiàgèyuè xiǎng qù Fēizhōu. (They would like to go to Africa next week.)

_____

4 Nǐmen zhègèxīngqī'èr wǎnshàng yào bú yào qù tīng yǎnchànghuì? (Are you guys going to listen to the concert this Tuesday evening?)

_____

D Where would your imaginary family members like to go? Answer the questions in Chinese.

1   2   3   4   5   6

1 Bàba xiǎng qù nǎ lǐ? _____

2 Māma xiǎng qù nǎ lǐ? _____

3 Gēge xiǎng qù nǎ lǐ? _____

4 Dìdi xiǎng qù nǎ lǐ? _____

5 Jiějie xiǎng qù nǎ lǐ? _____

6 Mèimei xiǎng qù nǎ lǐ? _____

 E You're going on a round-the-world trip and visiting each of the continents. Write a list of the continents you would like to visit and a list of countries you DON'T want to see + bonus task: state your reasons why.

Ex. Wǒ jīnnián dōngtiān yào qù Ōuzhōu, dànshì wǒ bù xiǎng qù Bōlán. Bōlán tiānqì tài lěng.
(This winter I am going to go to Europe, but I don't want to go to Poland. The weather in Poland is too cold.)

1 _____

2 _____

3 _____

4 _____

5 _____

Adverbs Of Frequency

A Match the time expressions to their English counterpart.

1 ___ měitiān   a next month

2 ___ shànggèyuè   b last week

3 ___ zhègèxīngqī   c this week

4 ___ měinián   d usually

5 ___ měigèyuè   e every year

6 ___ tōngcháng   f every month

7 ___ shànggèxīngqī   g last month

8 ___ xiàgèyuè   h every day

9 ___ měigèxīngqī   i every week

B Translate the following sentences from English to Chinese.

Ex: I have to work every Saturday. → Wǒ měigèxīngqīliù yào gōngzuò.

1 My girlfriend goes to the zoo every month. _____

2 Next Thursday I would like to go to a party. _____

3 The weather is very hot this week. _____

4 Where were you last month? _____

5 That student studies Chinese every day. _____

6 We eat dinner every evening. _____

C Unscramble the following sentences.

Ex: měigèxīngqī / Zhōngwén / kè / shàng / tā → Tā měigèxīngqī shàng Zhōngwén kè.

1 měitiān / qù / wǒmen / kāfēitīng / kāfēi / hē

_____

2 tāmen / měigèxīngqīwǔ / xǐhuān / chūqù / wǎnshàng

_____

3 shāngrén / nàgè / xǐhuān / měigèyuè / gāo'ěrfūqiú / dǎ / ma / ?

_____

4 jǐdiǎn / érzi / tōngcháng / nǐ / qǐchuáng / ?

_____

D Provide long answers to the questions using the words in parentheses.

Ex: Tā shénme shíhòu xǐhuān dǎ lánqiú? (every Thursday evening) →
Tā měigèxīngqīsì wǎnshàng xǐhuān dǎ lánqiú.

1 Nàgè lǎoshī shénme shíhòu shàng shùxué ke? (every Wednesday)

_____

2 Zhègè shāngrén shénme shíhòu yào zuò huǒchē qù shàngbān? (every morning)

_____

3 Nǐde xiǎohái tōngcháng jǐdiǎn qǐchuáng? (6 o'clock in the morning)

_____

4 Tāmende māma xǐ bù xǐhuān chī nánguā? (Yes)

_____

5 Nǐ nǎinai měinián xiàtiān xǐhuān qù nǎ lǐ? (Germany)

_____

E In Měiguó, Mike Lǎoshī's home country, Halloween is a big deal. Do you celebrate Halloween in your home country? If so, how do you celebrate? If not, do you celebrate a different holiday that is similar? Either way, write an e-mail to Mike Lǎoshī and do your best to describe the holiday. Where do you go? What do you eat / drink? Is it fun? Don't be afraid to use your dictionary!

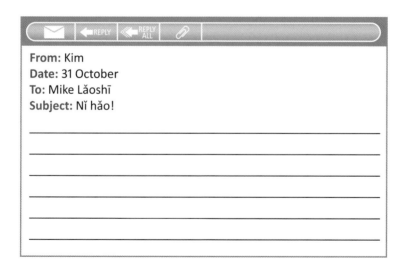

From: Kim
Date: 31 October
To: Mike Lǎoshī
Subject: Nǐ hǎo!

_____

_____

_____

_____

_____

_____

Subject + Place + Action 1

A Since most of this vocabulary has been introduced in the past, I'm going to assume that matching will be too easy for you. Thus, I'm going to have you simply write the translation of the following vocabulary words!

1 shūfáng _____

2 wòshì _____

3 kètīng _____

4 zhuō mí cáng _____

5 cèsuǒ _____

6 fángjiān _____

7 yóujú _____

8 shūdiàn _____

B Provide long answers using the words in parentheses.

Ex: Nǐ nǚ'ér zài nǎ lǐ xiě gōngkè? (in the dining room) → Wǒ nǚ'ér zài fàntīng (lǐ) xiě gōngkè.

1 Nǐ zài nǎ lǐ shuìjiào? (in the bedroom)

_____

2 Tā zài nǎ lǐ mǎi jīpiào? (at the airport)

_____

3 Nǐ bàba zài nǎ lǐ mǎi chēpiào? (at the train station)

_____

4 Xiǎoháizi zài nǎ lǐ wán zhuō mí cáng? (behind the house)

_____

5 Tāmen zài nǎ lǐ shū tóufǎ? (in the bathroom)

_____

6 Nàxiē gāozhōngshēng zài nǎ lǐ liànxí Zhōngwén? (at the library)

_____

C Unscramble the following sentences. Then translate the sentences into English.

Ex: zài / Pèishān / gōngzuò / shūdiàn → Pèishān zài shūdiàn gōngzuò.
Pèishān works at the bookstore.

1 zài / tā / kètīng / gāngqín / tán _____

2 nǐ / lā / zài / fángjiān / érzi / ma / xiǎotíqín / ? _____

3 xǐyīfáng / tàitai / wǒ / zài / xǐ / yīfú _____

4 ma / zài / shūfáng / mèimei / zuòyè / zuò / ? _____

D Look at the pictures and say where these people do the following activities. Use complete sentences to answer.

Ex: Tā zài túshūguǎn kàn shū.

1 _____ 2 _____ 3 _____ 4 _____

E You're responsible for interviewing a Chinese exchange student who is now living in your home country. Jot down some questions you might ask using our sentence patterns from this lesson.

Ex: Nǐ zài nǎ lǐ shàngkè? (Where do you attend class?)
Nǐ zài nǎ lǐ mǎi yīfú? (Where do you buy clothes?)

_____

_____

_____

_____

_____

_____

Subject + Place + Action 2

A Match the vocabulary words with their definitions.

1 ___ cháguǎn   **a** baseball field

2 ___ bówùguǎn   **b** teahouse

3 ___ lǚguǎn   **c** restaurant

4 ___ cānguǎn   **d** motel

5 ___ túshūguǎn   **e** parking lot

6 ___ shìchǎng   **f** market

7 ___ mǎi cài   **g** buy groceries

8 ___ bàngqiúchǎng   **h** museum

9 ___ tíngchēchǎng   **i** casino

10 ___ dǔchǎng   **j** library

B Provide long answers to the following using the words in parentheses.

Ex: Lǚguǎn zài nǎ lǐ? (across from the school) → Lǚguǎn zài xuéxiàode duìmiàn.

1 Dǔchǎng zài nǎ lǐ? (to the right of the teahouse)

   _____

2 Shìchǎng zài nǎ lǐ? (to the left of the library)

   _____

3 Tíngchēchǎng zài nǎ lǐ? (below the museum)

   _____

4 Cānguǎn zài nǎ lǐ? (behind the baseball field)

   _____

5 Cháguǎn zài nǎ lǐ? (across from the university)

   _____

6 Gāozhōng zài nǎ lǐ? (in front of the post office)

   _____

C Translate the following sentences from English to Chinese.

Ex: She likes to drink coffee at the coffee shop. → Tā xǐhuān zài kāfēitīng hē kāfēi.

1 I like to buy groceries at the market. _____

2 They would like to eat breakfast at the restaurant. _____

3 We like to play baseball at the baseball field. _____

4 Lily likes to study math at the library. _____

D Find the errors in the following translations and give the correct translations.

Ex: Nàgè nǚrén zài dǔchǎng shàngbān. (She works at the bank.) → She works at the casino.

1 Zhèxiē dàxuéshēng hěn xǐhuān zài diànyǐngyuàn kàn diànyǐng. (These high school students really like to watch movies at the movie theater.)

_____

2 Nàxiē gāozhōngshēng xiǎng yào zài cānguǎn chī wǔcān. (Those high school students would like to eat dinner at the restaurant.)

_____

3 Wǒde chēzi bú zài tíngchēchǎng lǐ. (My car is in the parking lot.)

_____

4 Nàgè nánrén xǐhuān zài cháguǎn hē lǜchá. (That man likes to drink black tea at the teahouse.)

_____

5 Zhègè nǚshēng zài yóujú gōngzuò. (This young woman works at the bank.)

_____

6 Zhègè nánshēng xǐhuān zài shūfáng zuò zuòyè. (This young man likes to cook in the study.)

_____

E 92.01 Listen to the following sentences and fill in the blanks with the words you hear.

1 _____ zài nǎ lǐ?

   Tā zài wǒmen jiāde _____.

2 Lily zài nǎ lǐ _____?

   Tā zài _____.

3 _____ zài nǎ lǐ?

   Tā zài cānguǎnde _____.

4 Tā zài nǎ lǐ _____?

   Tā zài _____.

Time And Place

A Are your new vocabulary words matched correctly? Write out the correct translations if you spot any mistakes.

1 niúpái – steak _____

2 kǎoròu – to work out _____

3 hòuyuàn – classroom _____

4 jiànshēnfáng – the gym _____

5 jiànshēn – to grill; to barbecue _____

6 tǐyùguǎn – chess _____

7 jiàoshì – backyard _____

8 xiàngqí – gymnasium _____

B Choose the words that make sense.

Ex: Nǐ xiǎng (kǎo) / hē shénme ròu?

1 Gēge yào qù **jiànshēnfáng / cānguǎn** zuò yùndòng.

2 Nǐde háizi xǐ bù xǐhuān wán **niúpái / xiàngqí**?

3 Xuéshēng zài **tǐyùguǎn / bówùguǎn** shàng tǐyù kè ma?

4 Gāozhōngde **jiàoshì / jiànshēn** dà bú dà?

5 Zhèzhī gǒu xǐhuān zài **hòuyuàn / jiàoshì** pǎo.

6 Wǒ tōngcháng bù chī ròu dànshì wǒ hěn xǐhuān chī **niúpái / xiàngqí**.

C When it gets close to the New Year, Mike Lǎoshī likes to try to get healthier. Create sentences about recommendations for a healthier lifestyle.

First, though, translate Mike Lǎoshī's habits now:

1 Mike Lǎoshī měitiān zǎoshàng hē kělè. _____

2 Mike Lǎoshī měitiān wǎnshàng hē píjiǔ. _____

3 Mike Lǎoshī měitiān chī bīngqílín. _____

4 Mike Lǎoshī měitiān xiàwǔ kàn diànshì. _____

5 Mike Lǎoshī měitiān wǎnshàng wán diàndòng yóuxì. _____

Now, what must Mike Lǎoshī do to be healthier?

Ex: Mike Lǎoshī měitiān zǎoshàng yào hē shuǐ. (Mike Lǎoshī must drink water every morning.)

Mike Lǎoshī měitiān xiàwǔ yào chī shūcài. (Mike Lǎoshī must eat vegetables every afternoon.)

6 _____

7 _____

8 _____

9 _____

10 _____

D Translate the following sentences.

Ex: Xiàngqí hǎo bù hǎowán? → Is (playing) chess fun?

1 Nǐ měitiān zǎoshàng qù jiànshēnfáng ma? _____

2 Nàgè niúpái hǎo bù hǎochī? _____

3 Nǐde nánpéngyǒu huì bú huì kǎoròu? _____

4 Tāde nǚpéngyǒu zài bú zài tǐyùguǎn? _____

5 Chén Lǎoshī zài tāde jiàoshì lǐ ma? _____

Review Of Time And Place

A **Given the clue, write the new vocabulary word in the blank.**

lǚxíng	májiàng	dìlǐkè	yóuyǒngchí	kāfēitīng
jiāoshū	huáxuě	tàijí	huāyuán	

1 If you want to be a teacher, I hope you know how to _____.

2 People who often explore other parts of the world must enjoy _____.

3 One of the most popular games in China is _____.

4 A popular martial art is called _____.

5 You plant flowers in your _____.

6 Take a _____ if you want to know more about geography.

7 Go swimming in the _____.

8 Drink coffee or have a scone in the _____.

9 Hopefully there is snow on the ground if you want to _____.

B **Given the question, write the short answer (one or two words) using the words in parentheses. Then translate the questions into English.**

Ex: Q: Nǐ nǎinai xǐhuān dǎ tàijí ma? (Yes)   **A:** Xǐhuān.

1 **Q:** Tāde huāyuán piào bú piàoliàng? (It's beautiful.)   **A:** _____

2 **Q:** Nǐmen jǐdiǎn yào shàng dìlǐkè? (ten o'clock)   **A:** _____

3 **Q:** Nǐ xiǎng bù xiǎng dǎ májiàng? (Yes)   **A:** _____

4 **Q:** Tāmen yào qù yóuyǒngchí ma? (Yes)   **A:** _____

5 **Q:** Xiànzài nǐmen zài kāfēitīng ma? (No)   **A:** _____

6 **Q:** Tāde xiǎohái huì bú huì huáxuě? (No)   **A:** _____

C **Translate the following two-verb sentences from Chinese to English.**

Ex: Wǒ měitiān wǎnshàng xǐhuān zài jiā lǐ kàn diànshì. → I like to watch TV at home every evening.

1 Xiāofángyuán tōngcháng xǐhuān zài kāfēitīng hē kāfēi. _____

2 Jǐngchá měigèxīngqīyī zài jiànshēnfáng yóuyǒng. _____

3 Nàgè chúshī měitiān yào zài cānguǎn zuòfàn. _____

4 Zhègè yīshēng xǐhuān zài yīyuàn gōngzuò. _____

D **94.01 Fill in the blanks with the missing time or place words.**

1 Tāmen _____ zài Fǎguó huáxuě.

2 Nàxiē dàxuéshēng _____ zài jiǔbā chī pīsà ma?

3 Wǒde wàipó měinián chūntiān zài _____ zhònghuā.

4 Zhègè nǚshēng xiàgèxīngqīliù yào zài _____ chànggē.

5 Nàgè shāngrén _____ zài lǚguǎn shuìjiào.

6 Zhèxiē nánshēng xǐhuān zài qiúchǎng _____ .

E **Someday your children will wonder what you used to do on a daily / weekly / monthly / yearly basis. Write a brief journal entry in which you describe some of your routines.**

I'll get you started:

Ex: Wǒ měitiān wǎnshàng kàn *Chinese with Mike*.
(Every evening I watch *Chinese with Mike*.)

_____

_____

_____

_____

_____

Lesson 95

Lesson **95**

Time And Place Questions

A Choose the vocabulary word that makes the most sense.

1 Hòutiān shì **Gǎnēnjié / zúqiúchǎng** ma?

2 Wǒ zài **zúqiúchǎng / bàngqiúchǎng** tī zúqiú.

3 Wǒde **gāozhōng / kǎoshì** yǒu 500 gè xuéshēng.

4 Tā xǐhuān qù nǎ lǐ **yóuyǒngchí / mǎi** dōngxī?

5 Nǐ jīntiān wǎnshàng yào zuò **huāyuán / zuòyè** ma?

6 Nǐmen jǐdiǎn yào qù **gōngkè / kāihuì**?

7 Tāmen zài **bàngōngshì / tàijí** shàngbān.

B Translate the following sentences into Chinese.

Ex: We would like to play mahjong in the living room tomorrow evening. →
Wǒmen míngtiān wǎnshàng xiǎng zài kètīng dǎ májiàng.

1 I like to play soccer at the soccer field every afternoon.

_____

2 When do you guys like to swim at the swimming pool?

_____

3 What time does he have to attend geography class at high school?

_____

4 Where does she plant flowers every spring?

_____

C Use the time words in parentheses to provide long answers to the following questions.

Ex: Tāmen shénme shíhòu zài jiànshēnfáng jiànshēn? (every morning) →
Tāmen měitiān zǎoshàng zài jiànshēnfáng jiànshēn.

1 Bàba jǐdiǎn zài bàngōngshì kāishǐ kāihuì? (8:00 in the morning)

_____

2 Māma xīngqījǐ zài chāojí shìchǎng mǎi cài? (Tuesday)

_____

3 Nǐ jǐdiǎn zài biànlì shāngdiàn mǎi dōngxī? (6:00 in the evening)

_____

4 Nàgè xuéshēng jǐyuè zài xuéxiào kǎoshì? (May)

_____

70   *Chinese with Mike* Advanced Beginner to Intermediate Activity Book   **Lesson 95** Time And Place Questions

D Use the place words in parentheses to provide long answers to the following questions.

Ex: Nǐ jīntiān yào zài nǎ lǐ yóuyǒng? (the swimming pool) →
Wǒ jīntiān yào zài yóuyǒngchí yóuyǒng.

1 Nǐde háizi měitiān wǎnshàng zài nǎ lǐ xiě gōngkè? (in the kitchen)

_____

2 Tā měigèxīngqī zài nǎ lǐ kǎoròu? (at his friend's house)

_____

3 Tāmen xīngqīsān yào zài nǎ lǐ shuìjiào? (at the motel)

_____

4 Māma měigèxīngqīsì zài nǎ lǐ xǐ yīfú? (at the cleaners)

_____

E You are Mike Lǎoshī's personal assistant. If you want to keep your job, translate some of his routines for the benefit of his Chinese PR team.

1 Mike Lǎoshī měitiān zǎoshàng shíyīdiǎn qǐchuáng.

2 Mike Lǎoshī měitiān wǎnshàng xǐhuān zài jiànshēnfáng jiànshēn.

3 Mike Lǎoshī měigèxīngqīsān xǐhuān zài yóuyǒngchí yóuyǒng.

4 Mike Lǎoshī měigèyuè xǐhuān chūguó.

5 Mike Lǎoshī měitiān wǎnshàng shídiǎn shuìjiào.

1 _____

2 _____

3 _____

4 _____

5 _____

Yě And Hé

A Put your new vocabulary words into two columns: food and places.

hànbǎo	Zhōngguóchéng	péigēn	gāo'ěrfūqiúchǎng	dàn
chāojí shìchǎng	shǔtiáo	jiāyóuzhàn	pīsà	règǒu

Food	Places

B Translate the following sentences from English to Chinese.

Ex: I want to eat corn and potatoes. → Wǒ yào chī yùmǐ hé tǔdòu.

1 My son likes to play baseball and basketball.

_____

2 Do you want to order a hot dog and a hamburger?

_____

3 My son and I have to go to the gas station.

_____

4 Dad would like to go to Italy and Spain.

_____

5 Is your husband going to order eggs and French fries?

_____

C Answer the questions with "shéi" using the words in parentheses.

Ex: Shéi yào dǎ pīngpāngqiú hé yǔmáoqiú? (Lily) → Lily yào dǎ pīngpāngqiú hé yǔmáoqiú.

1 Shéi huì tán jítā hé gāngqín? (My older brother) _____

2 Shéi xiǎng qù Táiwān hé Xīnjiāpō? (Her older sister) _____

3 Shéi yào diǎn hànbǎo hé shǔtiáo? (Mike Lǎoshī) _____

4 Shéi xǐhuān chī Zhōngguó cài hé Rìběn liàolí? (Jack) _____

D 96.01 Listen to the dialogue and answer the questions.

1 What does Pèishān have to do today? _____

2 What classes does Dàwèi have today? _____

3 Does Dàwèi like geography class? Why or why not? _____

4 Does Pèishān like geography class? Why or why not? _____

Hé And Gēn

A **Match the vocabulary words with their definitions.**

1 ___ sànbù		**a**	to run
2 ___ pūkèpái		**b**	to go for a walk; to take a walk
3 ___ kǎlāOK		**c**	to go fishing; to fish
4 ___ diàoyú		**d**	karaoke
5 ___ pǎobù		**e**	poker; playing cards
6 ___ tángguǒ		**f**	to go bowling
7 ___ dǎ bǎolíngqiú		**g**	candy

B **97.01 Listen and fill in the phrases you hear.**

1 Nǐ érzi _____ chàng kǎlāOK?

2 Tā jiějie _____ xǐhuān diàoyú.

3 Nàgè nǚshēng xiǎng yào diǎn péigēn _____.

4 Zhègè nánshēng _____ yào qù dǎ bǎolíngqiú.

C **Translate the following sentences into English.**

Ex: Nǐ bàba gēn shéi sànbù? → With whom does your dad go walking?

1 Wǒde lǜshī xiǎng chī báifàn gēn shūcài.

_____

2 Wǒ hé wǒde xiǎoháizi xiǎng qù mǎi cài hé jiāyóu.

_____

3 Nàxiē gāozhōngshēng měitiān xiàwǔ xǐhuān wán pūkèpái hé xiàngqí.

_____

4 Yīnwèi wǒ yéye měitiān sànbù gēn pǎobù, suǒyǐ tā hěn jiànkāng.

_____

5 Nàgè nǚshēng gēn shéi liànxí Zhōngwén?

_____

6 Zhègè nánshēng yào qù bàngōngshì gēn zúqiúchǎng.

_____

D Unscramble the following sentences. Note: Compound subjects/objects may be reversed.

Ex: xǐhuān / gēn / tā / dìdi / tā / diàoyú / qù → Tā gēn tā dìdi xǐhuān qù diàoyú.

1 gēn / hànbǎo / cānguǎnde / hǎo / shǔtiáo / bù / hǎochī / ?

_____

2 jǐdiǎn / hé / cài / qù / mǎi / xiǎng / nǐmen / jiāyóu / ?

_____

3 hé / wǎnshàng / tāmende / tóngxué / shíyī / yèdiàn / diǎn / yào / qù / tāmen

_____

4 nàgè / hěn / gēn / yáyī / nàgè / lǜshī / yǒuqián

_____

E Use "hé" or "gēn" and the verb given to make sentences about what you like doing.

Ex: qù → Wǒ hěn xǐhuān qù kāfēitīng hé (gēn) bówùguǎn.

chuān → Tā yào chuān T-xù hé (gēn) kùzi.

1 dǎ _____

2 wán _____

3 chī _____

4 hē _____

5 qù _____

6 kàn _____

Dōu And Yīqǐ

A Choose the word that makes the most sense in the following sentences.

1 Nǐmende **tángguǒ / Shèngdànshù** hǎo gāo!

2 Nǐ xiǎng bù xiǎng **yīqǐ / dōu** wán pūkèpái?

3 **Shèngdànjié / Shèngdànjié Kuài lè** shì jǐyuè jǐhào?

4 Tā **huàxué / jiànkāng** kè nán bù nán?

B Translate the following sentences into Chinese.

Ex: We are both extremely angry. (Wǒmen dōu hěn shēngqì.)

1 Do you want to go eat dinner together? _____

2 They are both college students. _____

3 Would you like to go fishing together? _____

4 Do you both live in London? _____

5 We both are going to go to China. _____

6 Are they together? _____

C Are the following sentences translated correctly? Write out the correct translation if you spot any errors.

Ex: Gǎnēnjié hé Shèngdànjié dōu shì jiérì. – Thanksgiving and Christmas are both holidays. (Correct)

1 Nǐmen xiǎng bù xiǎng yīqǐ shàng huàxué kè? – Would you guys like to take chemistry class together?

_____

2 Xiànzài tā hé tāde tóngshì zài yīqǐ ma? – Is he / she with his co-worker now?

_____

3 Nàgè nánshēng hé tāde fùmǔ zhù zài yīqǐ ma? – Does that young woman live with her parents?

_____

4 Wǒ yéye gēn wǒ wàigōng dōu hěn lǎo. – My grandfathers are both (very) old.

_____

5 Zhègè shùxué jiàoshòu hé nàgè huàxué jiàoshòu dōu chāo cōngmíng. – This math professor and that chemistry professor are both stupid.

_____

D Use the words in parentheses to answer the following questions.

Ex: Tāmen yào yīqǐ qù nǎ lǐ? (the beach) Tāmen yào yīqǐ qù hǎitān.

1 Nǐmen xiǎng yīqǐ zuò shénme? (play golf)

_____

2 Nǐ gēn shéi yào yīqǐ qù pàiduì? (my friend)

_____

3 Dàwèide mèimei hé tāde Zhōngwén lǎoshī míngtiān yào yīqǐ zuò shénme? (review Chinese)

_____

4 Nàgè yáyī hé tā lǎopó dōu shì Bōlánrén ma? (Yes)

_____

E Write a few sentences about your favorite holiday. How do you celebrate it? (Do your best! And don't be afraid to use your dictionary.)

Ex: Shí'èryuè èrshíwǔ hào shì Shèngdànjié. Wǒ gēn wǒde jiārén yīqǐ chī huǒjī hé huǒtuǐ. Kètīng lǐ yǒu Shèngdànshù. Wǒmen xǐhuān yīqǐ chàng Shèngdàn gē.

_____

_____

_____

_____

_____

Háiyǒu

A **Match the vocabulary words with their definitions. One word will be used more than once.**

1 ___ chūzūchē   **a** wedding

2 ___ hūnlǐ   **b** taxi

3 ___ hái méi   **c** or; still

4 ___ Yuènán   **d** in addition; furthermore; also

5 ___ háiyǒu   **e** Vietnam

6 ___ gōngchǎng   **f** a factory

7 ___ háishì   **g** not yet

8 ___ jìchéngchē   **h** still; yet

9 ___ hái

B **Translate the following sentences into Chinese.**

Ex: He / She has not eaten lunch yet. → Tā hái méi chī wǔcān.

1 Mom, Dad and I all want to eat spring rolls.

_____

2 Today I have to study French, math, and chemistry.

_____

3 When is the taxi going to come?

_____

4 Tomorrow we have to go to a wedding.

_____

5 The day after tomorrow I am going to play golf. Also, my friend and I are going to see a movie together.

_____

C Use the words in parentheses to complete the following sentences with "háiyǒu".

Ex: Shéi xiǎng qù mǎi dōngxī? (Lily, Jennifer, and I) → Lily, Jennifer, háiyǒu wǒ xiǎng qù mǎi dōngxī.

1 Shéi yào zuò zhètái chūzūchē? (My older brother, my older sister, and my younger sister)

_____

2 Zuótiān shéi zài gōngchǎng? (my boss, his secretary, and my co-workers)

_____

3 Tā yào diǎn shénme cài? (spring rolls, pork, and white rice)

_____

4 Míngtiān zǎoshàng Lily yào shàng shénme kè? (English, math, and computers)

_____

D Unscramble the following sentences. Note the punctuation where it has been included.

Ex: háiyǒu / xiǎng / xǐyīdiàn, / Jīntiān / shìchǎng / qù / jiāyóuzhàn / wǒ →
Jīntiān wǒ xiǎng qù xǐyīdiàn, shìchǎng háiyǒu jiāyóuzhàn.

1 diànshì / wòshì / tāde / chuáng, / yǒu / háiyǒu / shūguì,

_____

2 míngtiān / zuò / xiàwǔ / yào / jiā / gōngchē / qù / wǒde / péngyǒu / wǒ / . / Háiyǒu, / yīqǐ / wǎncān / tā / yào / wǒ / hé / chī

_____

3 xiānshēng, / wǒ / zuótiān / érzi / háiyǒu / nǚ'ér / dōu / Zhōngguóchéng / zài

_____

4 nǐmen / cài / chī / shíwù / xiǎng / háishì / Měiguó / Zhōngguó / ?

_____

E You are getting married next year. Write a short description of your perfect wedding. Where would you like to get married? Besides Mike Lǎoshī, who are you going to invite? What are you going to eat and drink? What else do you plan to do on your wedding day?

Ex: Yīnwèi míngnián wǒ yào jiéhūn, suǒyǐ wǒ hěn gāoxìng. Wǒ xiǎng yào yīgè hěn dàde hūnlǐ. Wǒde jiārén, péngyǒu, háiyǒu tóngxué dōu yào lái. Wǒ xiǎng yào yīgè hěn bàngde jiéhūn dàngāo.

_____

_____

_____

_____

_____

Word Order And Prepositional Phrases

A Match the vocabulary words to their definitions. Since this is the last lesson before my retirement, I'm throwing a lot at you, I know. Don't worry – you can handle it.

1 ___ liáotiān		**a**	to celebrate
2 ___ xīnnián		**b**	new year
3 ___ qìngzhù		**c**	to chat
4 ___ xiūchē		**d**	to meet
5 ___ jiànmiàn		**e**	to repair a car
6 ___ shàngxué		**f**	to attend school
7 ___ bāshì		**g**	Thailand
8 ___ lánqiúchǎng		**h**	California
9 ___ Jiāzhōu		**i**	a neighbor
10 ___ línjū		**j**	a bus
11 ___ jiàoliàn		**k**	coach (sports)
12 ___ wàiguórén		**l**	a bar
13 ___ jiǔbā		**m**	basketball court
14 ___ Tàiguó		**n**	foreigner

B Translate the following sentences.

Ex: Nàgè jìgōng měitiān gēn tāde tóngshì yìqǐ xiūchē. →
Every day that mechanic and his co-workers fix cars together.

1 Tāde fùmǔ míngnián qiūtiān xiǎng zài Jiāzhōu gēn tāde dìdi jiànmiàn.

_____

2 Lily měigèxīngqī xǐhuān zài lánqiúchǎng hé péngyǒu dǎ lánqiú.

_____

3 Nǐ jīntiān wǎnshàng yào gēn shéi yìqǐ qù yèdiàn?

_____

4 Wǒ měitiān xiàwǔ zài cháguǎn gēn wǒde hǎo péngyǒu liáotiān.

_____

C   Fill in the correct question word that corresponds to the following answers.

Ex: Tāmen ___xīngqījǐ___ yào zài gōngyuán gēn tóngxué jiànmiàn?
Tāmen xīngqīyī yào zài gōngyuán gēn tóngxué jiànmiàn.

1   Nǐmen _____ xiǎng qù Tàiguó lǚxíng?
Wǒmen sānyuè xiǎng qù Tàiguó lǚxíng.

2   Dàwèi hé Pèishān měitiān zǎoshàng zài _____ mǎi tángguǒ?
Dàwèi hé Pèishān měitiān zǎoshàng zài biànlì shāngdiàn mǎi tángguǒ.

3   Nǐ gēn _____ zài yīqǐ?
Wǒ gēn wǒ jiějie zài yīqǐ.

4   Nàxiē Zhōngwén lǎoshī měigèxīngqīwǔ zài bàngōngshì gēn _____ liáotiān?
Nàxiē Zhōngwén lǎoshī měigèxīngqīwǔ zài bàngōngshì gēn tóngshì liáotiān.

5   Lily měitiān _____ zài tíngchēchǎng tíngchē?
Lily měitiān liǎngdiǎn zài tíngchēchǎng tíngchē.

6   Nǐ bàba _____ zài jiànshēnfáng jiànshēn?
Wǒ bàba xīngqīsān zài jiànshēnfáng jiànshēn.

D   Are the following sentence parts in the correct order? If not, correct the word order, and write out the full sentences.

Ex: (Chúshī) (qiántiān) (zài cānguǎn) (ma)? → (Correct)

(Tā) (zuò jìchéngchē) (xīngqīsān hé xīngqīsì) (gēn tā nǚpéngyǒu yīqǐ). (Incorrect) →
Tā xīngqīsān hé xīngqīsì gēn tā nǚpéngyǒu yīqǐ zuò jìchéngchē.

1   (zài chúfáng) (zhègè nánshēng) (měitiān wǎnshàng) (gēn tā mèimei yīqǐ) (xǐwǎn).

_____

2   (Lilyde bàbamāma) (zài kètīng) (měigèxīngqītiān xiàwǔ) (xǐhuān) (gēn tāmende xiǎoháizi) (wán yóuxì).

_____

3   (Tā) (shàngbān) (zài gōngchǎng) (ma)?

_____

4   (Nǐmende jiàoliàn) (shénme shíhòu) (xǐhuān) (zài lánqiúchǎng) (gēn nǐmen) (liànxí dǎ lánqiú)?

_____

E   Time for more Facebook status updates! Using the patterns from Lesson 100 Exercise B of your Coursebook, let the world know about some of your daily routines.

Like • Comment • Share
👍 4 people like this

Ex: Dàwèi měitiān zǎoshàng zài wòshì gēn tā gēge yīqǐ xiě gōngkè.
Dàwèi měitiān wǎnshàng xǐhuān zài dìxiàshì tīng yīnyuè.

_____

_____

Write a comment...

Comparisons with Bǐ

A Match the new vocabulary words with their definitions.

1 ___ bǐ   **a** sour

2 ___ bù   **b** spicy

3 ___ shǒu   **c** MW for songs

4 ___ bēi   **d** a comparative particle

5 ___ kǔ   **e** MW for movies

6 ___ là   **f** bitter

7 ___ tián   **g** sweet

8 ___ suān   **h** MW for cups; glasses

B Unscramble the following sentences. (Note: Subjects may be reversed.)

Ex: nǎinai / bǐ / nǐde / nǐ / jiànkāng → Nǐde nǎinai bǐ nǐ jiànkāng. OR Nǐ bǐ nǐde nǎinai jiànkāng.

1 wǒ / bǐ / ǎi / wǒ / yéye _____

2 qióng / tóngxué / bǐ / tā / tāde _____

3 bǐ / gǒu / lǎo / wǒde / gǒu / tāde _____

4 zhèxiē / nàxiē / bǐ / diànshì / guì _____

C Translate the following sentences.

Ex: Wǒde nǚpéngyǒu bǐ nàgè nǚshēng piàoliàng. → My girlfriend is prettier than that young woman.

1 Tāde nánpéngyǒu bǐ zhègè nánshēng shuài. _____

2 Lily bǐ wǒ è. _____

3 Mèimei bǐ dìdi kě. _____

4 Zuótiān māma bǐ bàba shēngqì. _____

5 Tāmen bǐ wǒmen yǒuqián. _____

6 Nàgè nánrén bǐ nǐmen qióng. _____

D Fill in the blanks with a word that makes sense.

Ex: Wǒde chēzi bǐ nǐde chēzi _____kuài_____ .

1 Tùzi bǐ wūguī _____.

2 Zhèxiē yīfú bǐ nàxiē yīfú _____.

3 Zuò bāshì bǐ zuò fēijī _____.

4 Zhètái shǒujī bǐ wǒde _____.

5 Nǐ bǐ wǒ _____.

6 Mike Lǎoshīde shū bǐ nàběn Zhōngwén shū _____.

E Using the particle "bǐ", compare Mike Lǎoshī to your other teachers.

Ex: Mike Lǎoshīde kè **bǐ** tāmende kè yǒuqù. Mike Lǎoshīde yīfú **bǐ** tāmende yīfú kù (*cool*).
Mike Lǎoshīde shū **bǐ** tāmende shū hǎokàn. Mike Lǎoshī **bǐ** tāmen cōngmíng.

_____

_____

_____

_____

_____

Comparatives And Superlatives

A Look at the pictures and write comparative sentences using the words in parentheses.

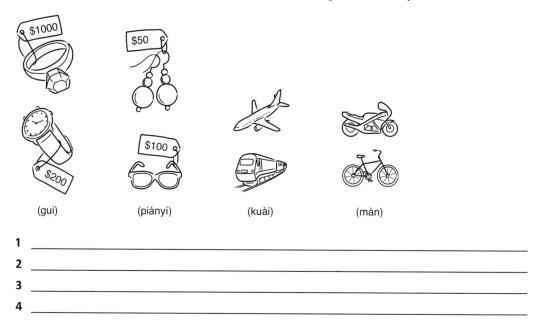

(gui)   (piányí)   (kuài)   (màn)

1 _____

2 _____

3 _____

4 _____

B Choose the word which makes the most sense in the following sentences.

1 Wǒde níngméngzhī **bǐ / zuì** nǐde suān.

2 Měiguóde yùmǐ **bǐ / zuì** tián.

3 Xióngmāo shì **bǐ / zuì** kě'àide dòngwù.

4 Huāshēng **bǐ / zuì** tǔdòu xiǎo.

5 Zhèbāo bàomǐhuā **bǐ / zuì** hǎochī.

6 Shēngwùxué hěn yǒuqù, **dànshì / bǐ** huàxué zuì yǒuqù.

7 Dìdi ài qìngzhù xīnnián yě ài qìngzhù shèngdànjié, dànshì tā **zuì / bǐ** ài qìngzhù wànshèngjié.

C Translate the following sentences.

Ex: Nàbāo huāshēng bǐ zhèbāo huāshēng piányí. →
That package of peanuts is cheaper than this package of peanuts.

1 Zhèwǎn chǎofàn bǐ nàwǎn báifàn hǎochī. _____

2 Shéi zuì yǒuqián? _____

3 Zuì hǎode hǎitān zài nǎ lǐ? _____

4 Wǒmende chēzi bǐ tāmende chēzi jiù. Dàwèide chēzi zuì jiù. _____

5 Nàgè nánshēng shì wǒ bānjí zuì cōngmíngde xuéshēng. _____

D 102.01 Listen to the conversation and fill in the blanks.

1 **Pèishān:** Nǐ zài zhǎo _____?

2 **Dàwèi:** Wǒ zài zhǎo _____ piányíde _____.

3 **Pèishān:** _____? Nǐ _____ mǎi xīnde ma?

4 **Dàwèi:** _____. Wǒ yào mǎi xīnde. Wǒde _____ hěn jiù.

5 **Pèishān:** Nǐ xiǎng mǎi shénme _____?

6 **Dàwèi:** Wǒ xiǎng mǎi _____. Huángsède _____ liàng.

7 **Pèishān:** Wǒ _____ xǐhuān huángsède _____ _____.

E Answer the following questions, based on the conversation.

1 What is Dàwèi shopping for? _____

2 Does he want to spend a lot of money for it? _____

3 What color does he like? _____

4 What color does Pèishān like more? _____

F Unscramble the following sentences. Note the punctuation where it has been included.

Ex: gē / Rìwén / bǐ / hǎotīng / gē / Yīngwén / . / Zhōngwén / gē / hǎotīng / zuì →
Yīngwén gē bǐ Rìwén gē hǎotīng. Zhōngwén gē zuì hǎotīng.

1 zhètái / xǐyījī / zuì / hǎoyòng

_____

2 Tāde / háizi / bǐ / wǒde / háizi / guāi / . / Lilyde / háizi / zuì / guāi

_____

3 nán / kè / Shēngwùxué / huàxué / bǐ / kè /. / Shùxué/ kè / nán / zuì

_____

4 shuǐguǒ / shì / Lánméi / zuì / tiánde

_____

Which One?

A Match the vocabulary words with their definitions.

1 ___ nǎ(yī)   a Sweden

2 ___ nǎguó   b Norway

3 ___ Nuówēi   c Finland

4 ___ Fēnlán   d MW for a pair of something

5 ___ Ruìdiǎn   e which country?

6 ___ chūshēng   f which?

7 ___ bǐsài   g competition

8 ___ shuāng   h to be born

B Translate the following "nǎ" phrases. When you're done, write out full questions using the "nǎ" phrases listed.

Ex: nǎběn shū → that book (Nǎběn shū shì nǐde? Which book is yours?)

1 nǎbēi lǜchá _____

2 nǎzhāng jīpiào _____

3 nǎzhāng zhǐ _____

4 nǎpíng niúnǎi _____

5 nǎgè nǚshēng _____

6 nǎzhī jī _____

7 nǎzhī qiānbǐ _____

8 nǎtiáo yú _____

C Answer the questions using the words in parentheses.

Ex: Nǎbù diànyǐng zuì hǎokàn? (This movie) → Zhèbù diànyǐng zuì hǎokàn.

1 Nǎbù chēzi zuì guì? (that black car) _____

2 Nǎgè jiàoshòu zuì hǎo? (Professor Lín) _____

3 Nǎtáng kè zuì yǒuqù? (history class) _____

4 Nǐ nǎyīnián chūshēng? (1991) _____

5 Nǐ nǎgèyuè yào qù Nuówēi? (August) _____

6 Nǎshuāng xiézi zuì hǎokàn? (this pair) _____

D Unscramble the following questions. When you're done, invent an answer to these questions and say them out loud.

Ex: guójiā / piàoliàng / zuì / nǎgè / ? → **Q:** Nǎgè guójiā zuì piàoliàng? (**A:** Zhōngguó zuì piàoliàng.)

1 nǎběn / zuì / kèběn / Fǎwén / hǎokàn / ?

_____

2 zuì / xǐwǎnjī / hǎoyòng / nǎtái / ?

_____

3 ruǎn / chuáng / zuì / nǎzhāng / ?

_____

4 bǐ / nǎzhī / piányí / zuì / ?

_____

E Think about your own life and answer the questions.

Ex: Nǐ kāi nǎbù chēzi? → Wǒ kāi Rìběn chēzi. (I drive a Japanese car.)

1 Nǐ xiǎng qù nǎgè guójiā? _____

2 Nǐ shì nǎguó rén? _____

3 Nǐ yào kàn nǎběn shū? _____

4 Nǐ xiǎng kàn nǎbù diànyǐng? _____

5 Nǐ xǐhuān nǎgè yǎnyuán? _____

Comparisons With Bǐjiào

A Put an X next to the words that use "jiàn" as a measure word. If the word does not use "jiàn" as its MW, fill in the blank with the word's correct MW.

Ex: yángzhuāng → X; māo → zhī

1 kùzi _____

2 shū _____

3 chènshān _____

4 kuàizi _____

5 xīzhuāng _____

6 bǐ _____

7 T-xù _____

8 qīngwā _____

9 chuáng _____

B Choose the correct word to complete the following sentences.

1 Nǎběn shū **bǐjiào / bǐ** hǎokàn?

2 Nǎinai yào mǎi liǎng **gè / jiàn** xīn(de) yīfú.

3 Nǎyījiàn máoyī **bǐ / bǐjiào** shūfú?

4 Wǒ yào chuān **T-xù / xīzhuāng** qù hūnlǐ.

5 Mèimei bù xǐhuān chuān **kùzi / yángzhuāng** qù jiànshēnfáng.

C Translate the following sentences.

Ex: Nǎbù diànyǐng bǐjiào hǎokàn? → Which movie is better?

1 Zhètiáo yú zuì cháng.

_____

2 Nǐ yǒu hěn duō máoyī. Nǎyījiàn zuì guì?

_____

3 Tāmen yǒu liǎngběn Zhōngwén zìdiǎn. Nǎyīběn bǐjiào hǎoyòng?

_____

4 Wǒ jiā yǒu sānbù chēzi. Wǒ bàbade chēzi zuì hǎokàn.

_____

5 Shìchǎng yǒu xiāngjiāo hé píngguǒ. Nǎgè bǐjiào tián?

_____

D Unscramble the following sentences.

Ex: zhèjiàn / fēicháng / guì / xīzhuāng → Zhèjiàn xīzhuāng fēicháng guì.

1 cháng / yángzhuāng / hǎo / nàjiàn _____

2 yīfú / nǎjiàn / shūfú / zuì / ? _____

3 xǐhuān / tàitai / nǐde / nǎshuāng /wàzi / ? _____

4 báibǎnbǐ / yòng / yào / lǎoshī / nǎzhī / nàgè / ? _____

E 104.01 Listen and fill in the blanks to complete the dialogues.

1a Nǎtái shǒujī _____ piányí?

1b _____ shǒujī bǐjiào piányí.

2 Zhèjiàn _____ bǐ nǐde chènshān _____.

3a _____ yīshēng _____ hǎo?

3b _____ yīshēng _____ hǎo.

4a Nǎbēi guǒzhī _____?

4b _____.

Preferences And Favorites

A Use the words in the word bank to complete the following sentences.

| bǐjiào xǐhuān | zuì xǐhuān | yǐnliào | Āijí | Yìndù |

1 Go to _____ if you want to see some pyramids.

2 If you've just run a mile, you may want a _____.

3 Go to _____ if you want to see the Taj Mahal.

4 Do you prefer to watch TV or *Chinese with Mike*? I _____ to watch *Chinese with Mike*.

5 My children enjoy watching movies, reading books, and surfing the Internet. However, they _____ playing video games.

B Given the answer, write the question using one of the following question words: "shénme", "nǎ lǐ", or "shénme shíhòu".

Ex: **A:** Tāmen zuì xǐhuān chī règǒu. → **Q:** Tāmen zuì xǐhuān chī shénme (shíwù)?

1 **A:** Wǒmen měitiān dōu dǎ zhuōqiú.

   Q: _____

2 **A:** Wáng Xiānshēng míngnián xiàtiān yào qù Yìndù.

   Q: _____

3 **A:** Chén Tàitai zài kāfēitīng hē yǐnliào.

   Q: _____

4 **A:** Wǒde nǚpéngyǒu bǐjiào xǐhuān chī pīsà.

   Q: _____

C Translate the following sentences.

Ex: Āijí zài Fēizhōu. → Egypt is in Africa.

1 Tā hěn xǐhuān māo kěshì tā zuì xǐhuān gǒu.

   _____

2 Wǒ měigèxīngqīliù zuì xǐhuān zài dìxiàshì dǎ zhuōqiú.

   _____

3 Nǐmen bǐjiào xǐhuān tǐyù kè háishì shēngwùxué kè?

   _____

4 Wǒde hǎo péngyǒu zuì xǐhuān chī Yìndù cài.

   _____

D What do your family members and friends like to do the most? Fill in the blanks with all the new vocabulary you've learned.

Ex: Wǒ mèimei zuì xǐhuān **mǎi yīfú** dànshì **wǒ jiějie** zuì xǐhuān **kàn shū**.

1 _____ zuì xǐhuān _____ dànshì _____ zuì xǐhuān _____.

2 _____ zuì xǐhuān _____ dànshì _____ zuì xǐhuān _____.

3 _____ zuì xǐhuān _____ dànshì _____ zuì xǐhuān _____.

4 _____ zuì xǐhuān _____ dànshì _____ zuì xǐhuān _____.

Gèng

A Match the vocabulary words to their definitions.

1 ___ (shòu)ruò   **a** kitten

2 ___ yìng   **b** even more

3 ___ ruǎn   **c** thin and weak

4 ___ gèng   **d** soft

5 ___ (qiáng)zhuàng   **e** table tennis; ping-pong; billiards (in mainland China)

6 ___ xiǎogǒu   **f** puppy

7 ___ zhuōqiú   **g** strong; powerful

8 ___ xiǎomāo   **h** hard (physically)

B Are the following translations correct? If not, write out the correct translations in the spaces provided.

Ex: This evening is even colder. (Zuótiān wǎnshàng gèng lěng.) → (Incorrect.)
　　Jīntiān wǎnshàng gèng lěng.

1 My maternal grandfather exercises every day. He is extremely strong. (Wǒ yéye měitiān yùndòng. Tā fēicháng shòuruò.)

　　_____

2 This girl doesn't like to eat. She is very weak. (Zhègè nǚhái bù xǐhuān chīfàn. Tā hěn qiángzhuàng.)

　　_____

3 Pencils are harder than brush pens. (Qiānbǐ bǐ máobǐ yìng.)

　　_____

4 Beds are softer than couches. (Chuáng bǐ shāfā yìng.)

　　_____

5 Kittens like to eat fish. (Xiǎomāo ài chī yú.)

　　_____

6 Kids are even naughtier than puppies. (Xiǎohái bǐ xiǎogǒu gèng wánpí.)

　　_____

7 Table tennis is even more difficult than baseball. (Bàngqiú bǐ zhuōqiú gèng xiǎo.)

　　_____

C Translate the following from Chinese to English.

Ex: Wǒ gèng shēngqì. → I am even angrier.

1 Nàgè lǜshī bǐ wǒ bàba gèng yǒuqián. _____

2 Lily bǐ tāde tóngxué gèng lǎnduò. _____

3 Huàxué bǐ shùxué gèng wúliáo. _____

4 Fàndiàn bǐ lǚguǎn gèng guì. _____

5 Nàzhī xiǎogǒu bǐ nàzhī xiǎomāo gèng kě'ài. _____

D Fill in the blanks with "bǐ," "bǐjiào," or "gèng". Some may have more than one correct answer.

Ex: Lily ___bǐ___ wǒ ___gèng___ cōngmíng.

1 Yǔmáoqiú _____ hǎowán.

2 Xiǎogǒu _____ xiǎomāo wánpí.

3 Dàwèi hěn ǎi dànshì tā dìdi _____ ǎi.

4 Wǒmen xǐhuān chī chǎofàn kěshì wǒmen _____ xǐhuān chī chǎomiàn.

5 Nǐ _____ xǐhuān hē kāfēi háishì chá?

E Make comparative sentences about people you know using "bǐ" and "gèng". Try to use all the new vocabulary that you've learned throughout this course.

Ex: Wǒde tóngxué bǐ wǒde nánpéngyǒu gèng cōngmíng.
(My classmate is even smarter than my boyfriend.)

1 _____

2 _____

3 _____

4 _____

5 _____

Yīyàng

A **Choose the best word from the word bank to complete each sentence.**

tiáo	dà	Zhījiāgē	lù	xiǎo	yīyàng

1 Nǐde tóufǎ hé wǒde tóufa _____ hēi.

2 Mike Lǎoshī shì _____ rén.

3 Tā hé tā péngyǒude jiǎo yīyàng _____.

4 Shīzi bǐ dàxiàng _____.

5 Zhè _____ yú hěn chòu.

6 Nàtiáo _____ mán cháng.

B **Translate the following expressions from English to Chinese using "zhè / nà" + MW + noun.**

Ex: those four sweaters → nàsìjiàn máoyī

1 these five pens _____

2 these two bowls of soup _____

3 those nine boys _____

4 these twelve bottles of beer _____

5 those two fish _____

C **Unscramble the following sentences and translate. (Note: Subjects may be reversed.) Do you agree with the statements? If not, state why ("Yīnwèi . . .")!**

Ex: hé / piàoliàng / Niǔyuēshì / yīyàng / Zhījiāgē. → Zhījiāgē hé Niǔyuēshì yīyàng piàoliàng. (Chicago is just as beautiful as New York.) – Disagree: Yīnwèi wǒ juéde Niǔyuēshì shì zuì piàoliàngde chéngshì. (Because I feel that New York City is the most beautiful city.)

1 hé / tóngxué / wǒde / wǒ / yīyàng

_____

2 zhèxiē / zhèxiē /gēn / tián / lánméi / yīyàng / cǎoméi

_____

3 nà / yīyàng / níngméng / liǎnggè / suān

_____

4 dà / zhèsāngè / yīyàng / rén

_____

D **Are the following translations correct? If not, write out the correct translation in the spaces provided.**

Ex: Nàsìzhāng chuáng yīyàng ruǎn. (Those four chairs are equally soft.) →
Incorrect – Those four beds are equally soft.

1 Tā gēn tā māma yīyàng. (He / She is just like his / her older sister.)

_____

2 Tāmen hé wǒmen yīyàng máng. (They are just as busy as we are.)

_____

3 Nàsānběn huàxué kèběn yīyàng nán. (Those four chemistry textbooks are equally difficult.)

_____

4 Zhèliǎngbù diànyǐng yīyàng yǒuqù. (Those two movies are equally interesting.)

_____

Review Of Comparisons

A Match the definitions from the word bank with the new vocabulary.

	soccer match	comparative particle	
which	the most	even more	the same

1 nǎ (yī) _____

2 bǐ _____

3 gèng _____

4 zuì _____

5 yīyàng _____

6 zúqiúsài _____

B Translate the following sentences.

Ex: I am even dumber than my younger brother. → Wǒ bǐ wǒ dìdi gèng bèn.

1 Nàxiē chūnjuǎn bǐ zhèxiē hǎochī. _____

2 Nǎyījiàn chènshān zuì shūfú? _____

3 Zhèsāngè nánshēng yīyàng shuài. _____

4 Shéi bǐjiào qiángzhuàng? _____

C 108.01 Listen to the following sentences and fill in the missing word.

1 Wǒmende _____ yīyàng dà.

2 Nǐ gēn nǐde jiějie yīyàng _____ ma?

3 Wǒde nǚpéngyǒu bǐ wǒ _____ ǎi.

4 Kàn zúqiúsài _____.

5 Zhèjiàn wàitào _____ wēnnuǎn.

6 Nǎpíng niúnǎi _____ piányí?

D Unscramble the following sentences. (Note: Subjects may be reversed.)

Ex: gēn / xiānshēng / yīyàng / nǐ / nǐ / dà / ma / ? → Nǐ xiānshēng gēn nǐ yīyàng dà ma?

1 diànnǎo / bǐjìběn / zhèliǎngtái / ma / hǎoyòng / yīyàng / ?

_____

2 érzi / wǒ / bǐ / dà / nǚ'ér / wǒ

_____

3 bǐjiào / lánsède / yángzhuāng / zhèjiàn / hǎokàn

_____

4 rén / shì / nánshēng / nǎguó / nàxiē / ?

_____

The Particles A, Wā And Ba

A Choose the most appropriate particle from the word bank to complete each sentence.

| ne | a | de | ma | ba | wā | bǐ |

1 Hǎo _____!

2 _____! Hǎo bàng!

3 Nǐ hǎo _____?

4 Wǒ hěn hǎo. Nǐ _____?

5 Zhège píngguǒ shì wǒ _____.

6 Nǐmen qù xǐ shǒu _____.

7 Jīntiān _____ zuótiān lěng.

B Unscramble the following sentences paying attention to the punctuation provided.

Ex: hǎo / Wā! / a! /gāo / nǐ → Wā! Nǐ hǎo gāo a!

1 hěn / diànyǐng / zhèbù / wúliáo /. / zǒu / wǒmen / ba

_____

2 shíyīdiǎn / shì / wǎnshàng / xiànzài / . / wǒmen / qù / ba / shuìjiào

_____

3 nǐ / chī / bù / xǐ / xǐhuān / dàngāo? / a! / xǐhuān

_____

4 wǎnshàng / xīngqīliù / nǐmen / xiǎng / yèdiàn / wǒ / ma / qù / gēn / yīqǐ / ? / a! / xiǎng

_____

C **109.01** Listen to the following pairs of sentences and fill in the blanks with the words you hear.

1 Wǒ érzi(de) shēntǐ bù shūfú. _____ tā qù kàn yīshēng _____.

2 Nǐ xiǎng bù xiǎng qù kàn _____? Xiǎng _____!

3 Bú yào wán _____. Nǐ qù zuò nǐde zuòyè! Hǎo _____.

4 Zhè shì wǒde nǚpéngyǒu. _____! Tā hǎo piàoliàng _____!

5 Zhètáng kè hǎo wúliáo. Wǒmen zǒu _____!

6 Yīnwèi wǒde nánpéngyǒu bù xǐhuān xǐzǎo, suǒyǐ tā hěn chòu! Qù zhǎo xīnde _____.

D Translate the following suggestions.

Ex: Let's go to the new movie theater! → Wǒmen qù xīnde diànyǐngyuàn ba!

1 Let's go buy a bottle of champagne. _____

2 Let's eat breakfast at a restaurant tomorrow morning. _____

3 Let's go play golf. _____

4 Let's take a plane to California. _____

The Future Tense

A Write the meaning of your new vocabulary words. Challenge: can you make one monster sentence using all of these words?

1 huì _____

2 xià yǔ _____

3 bú huì _____

4 xià xuě _____

_____

B Translate the following sentences. (Subjects and time expressions may be reversed.)

Ex: Tomorrow I will go shopping. → Míngtiān wǒ huì qù mǎi dōngxī. /
Wǒ míngtiān huì qù mǎi dōngxī.

1 The day after tomorrow she will attend biology class. _____

2 Next year we will go to Italy. _____

3 They will not eat dinner at the restaurant this evening. _____

4 Lily won't play soccer next weekend. _____

C Given the answer, write the question.

Ex: A: Míngtiān wǒ huì qù túshūguǎn. → **Q:** Míngtiān nǐ huì qù nǎ lǐ?

1 **A:** Huì. Tā míngnián huì bìyè.

Q: _____

2 **A:** Bú huì. Tāmen hòunián bú huì bānjiā.

Q: _____

3 **A:** Wǒmen xīngqīsān wǎnshàng huì chī niúròu chǎofàn hé shūcài.

Q: _____

4 **A:** Huì. Wǒde xiǎoháizi xiàgèxīngqī huì fàng shǔjià.

Q: _____

D Unscramble the following sentences.

Ex: wǒ / lái / nánpéngyǒu / xiàgèyuè / jiějiede / huì / jiā / wǒmen →
Wǒ jiějiede nánpéngyǒu xiàgèyuè huì lái wǒmen jiā.

1 nǚshēng / nàgè / 2016 nián / jiéhūn / huì _____

2 hòunián / nánrén / zhègè / bú / bìyè / huì _____

3 jīntiān / huì / xiàyǔ / xiàwǔ / bú _____

4 xiàxuě / bú / huì / huì / xiàgèxīngqīyī / ? _____

E Look at the pictures and use "huì" to form sentences about what these people will do at the given times.

(John/next Saturday)　　(Mary/next month)　　(Lily/tomorrow)　　(Steve/this evening)

1 _____

2 _____

3 _____

4 _____

Yǐqián (General Past)

A Vocabulary: Choose the word that best fits each definition.

1 Before; in the past is **xiànzài / yǐqián**.

2 Now; at the moment is **yǐqián / xiànzài**.

3 To think; to feel is **juéde / yào**.

4 To wish; to want is **xiǎng / juéde**.

5 To live is **jiā / zhù**.

B Answer the questions using the answers in parentheses.

Ex: Yǐqián nǐ zuì xǐhuān chī shénme? (French fries) → Yǐqián wǒ zuì xǐhuān chī shǔtiáo.

1 Yǐqián tā zuì xǐhuān hē shénme? (orange juice)

   _____

2 Yǐqián tāmen zài nǎ lǐ yùndòng? (at the gym)

   _____

3 Yǐqián nǐmen shénme shíhòu qù lǚxíng? (every summer)

   _____

4 Yǐqián nǐ mèimei xiǎng zhù (zài) nǎ lǐ? (Paris)

   _____

C Translate the following sentences. (Note: Subjects and time expressions may be reversed.)

Ex: Where did he used to attend Chinese class? → Tā yǐqián zài nǎ lǐ shàng Zhōngwén kè?

1 Did your older sister enjoy playing badminton in the past?

   _____

2 Where did you guys used to live?

   _____

3 Did you use to go to bed at nine o'clock in the evening?

   _____

4 Was Lily extremely busy in the past?

   _____

D **Unscramble the following sentences. (Note: Subjects and "yǐqián" may be reversed.)**

Ex: juéde / wǒ / yǐqián / huàxué / nán / hěn. → Yǐqián wǒ juéde huàxué hěn nán. OR
Wǒ yǐqián juéde huàxué hěn nán.

1 wǒ / jiéhūn / yǐqián / bù / xiǎng / nǚpéngyǒu _____

2 nánpéngyǒu / tā / yǐqián / hěn / xiǎng / Mòxīgē / qù _____

3 yǐqián / nánshēng / yǐqián / pàng / hěn / nàgè _____

4 zhègè / fēicháng / yǐqián / nǚshēng / shòu _____

E **Fill in the blanks with words and phrases about your secret past life.**

Ex: Wǒ yǐqián bù xǐhuān kàn shū. (In the past, I didn't like to read.)

1 Wǒ yǐqián xǐhuān kàn _____

2 Wǒ yǐqián hěn xǐhuān dǎ _____

3 Yǐqián wǒ xiǎng zhù zài _____

4 Wǒ yǐqián bù xǐhuān chī _____

5 Wǒ yǐqián bù xǐhuān hē _____

6 Wǒ yǐqián hěn xiǎng qù _____

7 Wǒ yǐqián fēicháng xǐhuān _____

Yǐhòu (General Future)

A Are the new vocabulary words matched correctly? If you spot any errors, fill in the blanks with the correct word.

Ex: jiéhūn – to live → Incorrect – to get married

1 yǐhòu – after; in the future _____

2 líhūn – to get married _____

3 dāng – to wait _____

4 zuò – yesterday _____

5 duì – yes; right; correct _____

6 xīnlǐ yīshēng – dentist _____

B Translate the following sentences.

Ex: Wǒ yǐhòu huì zhù zài Lúndūn. → I will live in London in the future.

1 Tā yǐhòu bú huì gōngzuò. _____

2 Nǐmen yǐhòu yào bú yào mǎi xīnde chēzi? _____

3 Yǐhòu tāmen huì zhù zài yīqǐ. _____

4 Lín Jiàoshòu yǐhòu huì zhǎo bǐjiào guìde gōngyù. _____

C Answer the questions using the words in parentheses.

Ex: Nàgè yáyī yǐhòu huì qù nǎ lǐ? (India)

1 Zhègè yǎnyuán yǐhòu huì jiéhūn ma? (No)

_____

2 Tā nǚpéngyǒu yǐhòu xiǎng dāng lǜshī ma? (Yes)

_____

3 Nǐ yǐhòu huì mài zhèběn shū ma? (No)

_____

4 Nǐ bàba yǐhòu xiǎng qù nǎ lǐ lǚxíng? (Norway and Sweden)

_____

D Unscramble the following sentences.

Ex: dāng / yǐhòu / tā / chúshī / xiǎng → Tā yǐhòu xiǎng dāng chúshī. OR Yǐhòu Tā xiǎng dāng chúshī.

1 huì / yǐhòu / wǒ / dài / kàn /qù / nǐ / yǎnchànghuì

_____

2 kàn / yǐhòu / bú / huì / wǒmen / tāmen/ qù / gējù / dài

_____

3 nǐmen / bú / huì / yǐhòu / wǒmende / huì / bàngōngshì / lái / ?

_____

4 huì / lǎoshī / zhèxiē / yǐhòu / wǒmen / jiāo

_____

E You've just stumbled across one of your old letters to a pen pal in which you were contemplating your future plans. What did you want to be? Where did you want to go? What did you want to do? Write your answers in the space provided.

> **Ex:** Yīnwèi wǒ yǐhòu xiǎng dāng yǎnyuán suǒyǐ wǒ huì zhù Luòshānjī. Wǒ yǐhòu huì hěn yǒumíng, yě huì hěn yǒuqián. Wǒ xiǎng mǎi yīgè hěn dàde fángzi. Fángzide hòumiàn yǒu yīgè hěn piàoliàngde yóuyǒngchí.

. . . De Shíhòu (When; At the Time)

A Match the following words with their definitions.

1	___ de shíhòu	**a**	sunglasses
2	___ hǎibiān	**b**	strict
3	___ zuò mèng	**c**	boss
4	___ tángguǒ	**d**	the seaside
5	___ yángé	**e**	popcorn
6	___ Táiběi	**f**	Shanghai
7	___ Shànghǎi	**g**	to dream; to have a dream
8	___ mà(rén)	**h**	childhood
9	___ huílái	**i**	to arrive
10	___ dào	**j**	to come back; to return
11	___ bàomǐhuā	**k**	to scold; yell at; curse (someone)
12	___ lǎobǎn	**l**	candy
13	___ tàiyáng yǎnjìng	**m**	when; at / during the time when . . .
14	___ xiǎo(de) shíhòu	**n**	Taipei

B Choose the word that best completes the following sentences. Construct your own sentences with the word you DIDN'T use, and say them out loud, paying close attention to your pronunciation.

Ex: Tā (lǎobǎn) / tángguǒ bǐjiào yángé. → Tángguǒ bú jiànkāng. (Candy is not healthy.)

1 Wǒ xǐhuān zài diànyǐngyuàn chī **lǎobǎn / bàomǐhuā**.

2 **Táiběi / Shànghǎi** bú zài Táiwān.

3 Yīnwèi jīntiān tàiyáng hěn dà, suǒyǐ wǒ yào dài wǒde **hǎibiān / tàiyáng** yǎnjìng.

4 Nǐ bàba xīngqījǐ **huílái / xiǎo(de) shíhòu**?

C Translate the following sentences.

Ex: Lily xiǎode shíhòu hěn xiǎng dāng lǎoshī. →
When Lily was a child, she really wanted to become a teacher.

1 Tā zài jiāde shíhòu bù xǐhuān xiě gōngkè.

_____

2 Wǒ hé wǒde lǎopó zài yīqǐde shíhòu xǐhuān tīng yīnyuè.

_____

3 Tāmen lǚxíngde shíhòu zhù (zài) lǚguǎn.

_____

4 Mary hé John chī pīsàde shíhòu xǐhuān hē kělè.

_____

D Think about your own life. What do you like to do in the following situations?

Ex: Wǒ zài gōngyuánde shíhòu → Wǒ zài gōngyuánde shíhòu xǐhuān sànbù.

1 Wǒ zài jiāde shíhòu _____.

2 Wǒ zài gōngzuòde shíhòu _____.

3 Wǒ zài kāichēde shíhòu _____.

4 Wǒ zài wàimiànde shíhòu _____.

5 Wǒ zài cāntīngde shíhòu _____.

Yǐqián (Before A Specific Time)

A **Match the new vocabulary words to their definitions.**

1 ___ yǐqián

2 ___ huíguó

3 ___ rènshì

4 ___ xiǎoshí

5 ___ kāfēiyīn

a an hour

b in the past; before (a specific event); ago

c caffeine

d to return to one's home country

e to meet; to know

B **Choose the best answer using your new vocabulary words.**

Ex: Tā rènshì wǒ ⟮**yǐqián**⟯ / **huíguó** zhù zài Xīnjiāpō.

1 Lǜchá yǒu méi yǒu **kāfēiyīn / xiǎoshí**?

2 Nàgè shāngrén shénme shíhòu yào **huíguó / rènshì**?

3 Tā **rènshì / kāixué** yǐqián yào mǎi làbǐ hé bǐjìběn.

4 Nǐ sāngè **rènshì / xiǎoshí** yǐqián zài nǎ lǐ?

5 Wǒ lǎopó **huíguó / rènshì** wǒ yǐqián méi yǒu gōngzuò.

C **Unscramble the following sentences. Translate the sentences into English when you are done.**

Ex: shàng / érzi / xiǎoshí / liǎnggè / wǒ / hái / zài / yǐqián / kè →
Wǒ érzi liǎnggè xiǎoshí yǐqián hái zài shàng kè.

1 nǐmen / kǎoshì / dàxué / yǐqián / shàng / yào

_____

2 kǎoshì / fùxí / yǐqián / yào / nǐmen

_____

3 bìyè / yǐqián / huíguó / huì / Dàwèi

_____

4 Pèishān / lǎogōng / tā / rènshì / yǐqián / nánguò / fēicháng

_____

D 114.01 **Listen to the dialogues and answer the following questions.**

1 What instrument was Pèishān really good at playing before she met Dàwèi?

_____

2 What instrument could Dàwèi not play before he met Pèishān?

_____

3 What will Pèishān do before she finishes work?

_____

4 What does Dàwèi like to do before he goes to work?

_____

E **Think you know about Mike Lǎoshī? Let's see if you do. Make up answers to the following statements about Mike Lǎoshī's past life.**

1 Mike Lǎoshī jiāo Zhōngwén yǐqián _____

2 Tā bìyè yǐqián _____

3 Tā zhù zài chēkù yǐqián _____

4 Mike Lǎoshī huí Měiguó yǐqián _____

Yǐhòu (After A Specific Time)

A Match the new vocabulary words to their definitions.

1 ___ kāixué		**a**	to arrive home
2 ___ huàn yīfú		**b**	to begin school
3 ___ shēng		**c**	to change (clothes)
4 ___ dàojiā		**d**	to give birth; to have a baby
5 ___ yǐhòu		**e**	in the future; after (a specific event)

B Choose the best answer using your new vocabulary words.

Ex: Tā jiéhūn yǐhòu huì (shēng) / dàojiā xiǎohái.

1 George **huàn yīfú / rènshì** yǐhòu yào qù shàngbān.

2 Wǒde háizi **kāixué / dàojiā** yǐhòu xǐhuān kàn diànshì.

3 Wǒ nǚ'ér shuìjiào **de shíhòu / yǐqián** huì zuò mèng.

4 Jīntiān wǒ lǎopó yào qù yīyuàn **shēng / dàojiā** xiǎohái.

C Translate the following sentences into English.

Ex: Yǐqián tā fēicháng ài yùndòng. → In the past, he / she really loved to exercise.

1 Wǒ yǐhòu xiǎng dāng xiāofángyuán. _____

2 Bàba dàojiā yǐhòu xǐhuān kàn qíusài. _____

3 Nǚrén shēng háizi yǐhòu yào xiūxi. _____

4 Shuìjiào yǐqián nǐ yào huàn yīfú. _____

5 Kāixué yǐhòu xúeshēng hùi hěn máng. _____

D Unscramble the sentences.

Ex: zū / wǒmen / yǐhòu / gōngyù / xīnde / mǎi / qù / yào / chuáng →
Wǒmen zū gōngyù yǐhòu yào qù mǎi xīnde chuáng.

1 Zhōngwén / dàxuéshēng / zhègè / yǐhòu / kāixué / kāishǐ / shàng / huì / kè

_____

2 nàgè / Fēnlán / bìyè / gāozhōngshēng / xiǎng / qù / lǚxíng / hé / Yīngguó / yǐhòu

_____

3 Bob / yǐhòu / xiǎohái / xiǎng / Lisa / hé / shēng / jiéhūn

_____

4 xǐhuān / yǐhòu / jiànshēn / wǒ / xǐzǎo

_____

E **Answer the questions using the words in parentheses.**

Ex: Tāmen huíjiā yǐhòu yào zuò shénme? (cook) → Tāmen huíjiā yǐhòu yào zuòfàn (zhǔfàn).

1 Nǐmen bìyè yǐhòu huì bú huì zhǎo gōngzuò? (Yes)

_____

2 Nǐ qǐchuáng yǐhòu xǐhuān zuò shénme? (play video games)

_____

3 Fred xiàkè yǐhòu yào qù nǎ lǐ? (go to the library)

_____

4 Nàgè yáyī xiàbān yǐhòu xǐhuān zuò shénme? (meet his friends)

_____

F **Mike Lǎoshī loves making resolutions. Unfortunately, he never sticks with them because they distract him from what he does best: teaching the world Chinese. In the spaces below, complete the sentences with your own resolutions for the given timeframes, and hopefully you'll have better luck than your amazing Chinese teacher.**

> **Ex:** Wǒ liùyuè yǐhòu xiǎng __bānjiā__ . → I would like to move (house) after the month of June.
>
> Resolutions:
>
> Wǒ yīgè yuè yǐhòu yào _____ .
>
> Wǒ xiàgèxīngqī yǐhòu xiǎng _____ .
>
> Wǒ yīyuè yīhào yǐhòu yào _____ .
>
> Wǒde shēngrì yǐhòu _____ .

Zĕnme (How?)

A Match the vocabulary words with their definitions.

1	___ lóngxiā		**a**	how
2	___ zĕnme		**b**	crab
3	___ yáokòngqì		**c**	lobster
4	___ wănglù		**d**	a remote control
5	___ liánluò		**e**	the Internet; a network
6	___ pángxiè		**f**	to get in touch with; to contact

B Translate the following sentences.

Ex: Tā zĕnme qù túshūguăn? → How does he / she get to the library?

1 Tāmen zĕnme dă yŭmáoqiú? _____

2 Nĭmen zĕnme zhŭ miàn? _____

3 Lĭ Lăoshī zĕnme jiāo Zhōngwén? _____

4 Nĭ zĕnme jiànshēn? _____

C 116.01 Fill in the blanks with the words you hear.

1 Nĭ érzi _____ qù shàngxué?

2 Zhègè nánrén zĕnme qù _____?

3 Nĭde mèimei zĕnme _____?

4 Xiànzài zài _____. Nĭ zĕnme qù _____?

D Answer the questions using the clues in parentheses.

Ex: Mèimei zěnme chī miàn? (uses a fork) → Mèimei yòng chāzi chī miàn.

1 Dìdi zěnme qù xuéxiào? (takes the bus)

_____

2 Gēge zěnme qù shàngbān? (drives a car)

_____

3 Jiějie zěnme mǎi jīpiào? (goes online)

_____

4 Nǐ zěnme xué Rìwén? (read a book)

_____

Zěnme (How? / Why?)

A "Zěnme" has two meanings: *how* and *why*. Fill in the blank with the correct translations of "zěnme" in the following sentences.

1 Nǐ zěnme qù gōngzuò? _____

2 Tāmen zěnme bù xué Zhōngwén? _____

3 Yéye zěnme bù shuō huà? _____

4 Nǐ(de) nǚpéngyǒu zěnme bù lái wǒde pàiduì? _____

5 Tā(de) nǎinai zěnme xǐ yīfú? _____

6 Wǒ(de) bàbamāma zěnme hái bù huí jiā? _____

B Look at the translations. Provide a correct translation of the sentences if you spot any errors.

Ex: Tā zěnme bú qù xuéxiào? (How does he / she get to school?) → Incorrect (How come he/she isn't going to school?)

1 Tāmen zěnme bú qù kàn qiúsài? (How come they don't go to watch the sports match?)

_____

2 Nǐmen zěnme bù lái wǒde shēngrì pàiduì? (Why aren't you guys coming to my wedding?)

_____

3 Nǐ zěnme bù gēn wǒ liánluò? (Why don't you keep in contact with me?)

_____

4 Tāmen zěnme bù chī lóngxiā? (Why don't they eat dragons?)

_____

C 117.01 Listen to the following pairs of sentences and answer the questions.

1 Dàwèi zěnme bú qù shàngkè?

_____

2 Pèishān zěnme bù xiǎng jiéhūn?

_____

3 Jīnnián Dàwèi zěnme bù néng bìyè?

_____

4 Míngnián nǐ zěnme bù xiǎng qù Yàzhōu?

_____

D Use the clues in parentheses to provide answers to the following questions.

Ex: Nàxiē xuéshēng zěnme bú qù bówùguǎn? (Because they would prefer to go to the zoo) →
Yīnwèi tāmen bǐjiào xiǎng qù dòngwùyuán.

1 Zhègè nánháizi zěnme bú zuò tāde zuòyè? (Because today he doesn't have homework)

_____

2 Nǐ érzi zěnme bù xǐhuān chī tángguǒ? (Because his teeth will hurt)

_____

3 Tāmende péngyǒu zěnme bù hē kělè? (Because cola is unhealthy)

_____

4 Tā zěnme bù xiǎng qù yóuyǒngchí? (Because it is cold today)

_____

E As a teacher, Mike Lǎoshī is used to hearing students' lame excuses for not getting their homework done. However, this particular student's excuse is that he doesn't have a Chinese dictionary. In the blanks below, list Mike Lǎoshī's four brilliant suggestions, the student's responses, and the final solution.

ML:	Nǐ zěnme bú zuò nǐde zuòyè?
Student:	Yīnwèi wǒ méi yǒu Zhōngwén zìdiǎn.
ML:	Nǐ zěnme bù shàngwǎng yòng wǎnglùde zìdiǎn?
Student:	Yīnwèi wǒ méi yǒu diànnǎo.
ML:	Nǐ zěnme bú qù túshūguǎn yòng diànnǎo?
Student:	Yīnwèi wǒ méi yǒu túshūguǎnde kǎ (library card).
ML:	Nǐ zěnme bú qù péngyǒu jiā yòng diànnǎo?
Student:	Yīnwèi wǒ méi yǒu péngyǒu.
ML:	Nǐ zěnme bù qù mǎi zìdiǎn?
Student:	Yīnwèi wǒ méi yǒu qián.
ML:	Hǎo. Wǒ gěi nǐ 10 kuài.

SUGGESTION 1: _____   RESPONSE 1: _____

SUGGESTION 2: _____   RESPONSE 2: _____

SUGGESTION 3: _____   RESPONSE 3: _____

SUGGESTION 4: _____   RESPONSE 4: _____

SOLUTION: _____

Zhème And Nàme

A Change the following statements into rhetorical questions using "zěnme zhème" or "zěnme nàme" using the words in parentheses.

Ex: Nǐ(de) háizi tài shòu. (zěnme zhème) → Nǐ(de) háizi zěnme zhème shòu?

1 Lín Tàitai de nǚ'ér chāo kě'ài. (zěnme zhème) _____

2 Lǐ Xiānshēngde érzi fēicháng cōngmíng. (zěnme nàme) _____

3 Mike Lǎoshī hěn qínláo. (zěnme zhème) _____

4 Zhègè zúqiúchǎng chāo dà. (zěnme nàme) _____

5 Wǒde dùzi hǎo tòng. (zěnme zhème) _____

B Translate the following sentences into Chinese. Use "zěnme nàme / zhème" pattern to translate the following sentences into Chinese.

Ex: Why are you so stubborn? → Nǐ zěnme nàme / zhème wángù?

1 Why is your girlfriend so busy? _____

2 How could she be this lazy? _____

3 Why does your boyfriend like fishing so much? _____

4 Why do your parents love watching TV this much? _____

C 118.01 Fill in the blanks with the answers you hear.

1 Tā zěnme nàme pàng?

_____

2 Nǐmen zěnme zhème ài kàn diànyǐng?

_____

3 Tā zěnme nàme xǐhuān jiāoshū?

_____

4 Nǐde chēzi zěnme nàme màn?

_____

D **Unscramble the following sentences.**

Ex: nàzhī / chòu / zěnme / nàme / gǒu / ? → Nàzhī gǒu zěnme nàme chòu?

1 zhègè / nàme / zěnme / dōngxī / nǚshēng / mǎi / xǐhuān / ?

_____

2 zěnme / nǚrén / nàgè / ài / zhème / màrén / ?

_____

3 gāo'ěrfūqiú / bàba / zěnme / nàme / nǐ / dǎ / xǐhuān / ?

_____

4 māma / tā / zěnme / yángé / nàme / ?

_____

E **People always ask: "Mike Lǎoshī zěnme nàme hǎo?" But now Mike Lǎoshī is looking for his best student. Is it you? "Nǐ zěnme nàme bàng?" Convince Mike Lǎoshī you're his best student and win a free *CWM* bandana!**

_____

_____

_____

_____

_____

Zěnmeyàng

A Match the vocabulary words with their definitions.

1 ___ bú cuò		**a**	MW for stores; shops
2 ___ hǎixiān		**b**	a program / show
3 ___ làngmàn		**c**	MW for rooms; spaces
4 ___ hǎokāi		**d**	"good ride"
5 ___ hǎoxiào		**e**	"good drive"
6 ___ hǎoqí		**f**	funny
7 ___ zěnmeyàng		**g**	not bad; pretty good
8 ___ jiémù		**h**	Chinese dumplings (food)
9 ___ jiā		**i**	romantic
10 ___ zuìjìn		**j**	recently; in the near future
11 ___ jiān		**k**	seafood
12 ___ shuǐjiǎo		**l**	how; how is it?; how about it?

B Are the following sentences translated correctly? Write out the correct translations if you spot any mistakes.

Ex: Nǐmen jīntiān wǎnshàng xiǎng kàn shénme jiémù?
(What TV show would you guys like to watch this evening?) → Correct

Tāmende fángzi zěnmeyàng? (How do you get to their house?) →
Incorrect – How is their house?

1 Nǐ lǎogōng zuìjìn zěnmeyàng? (How has your husband been recently?)

_____

2 Tā xǐ bù xǐhuān chī zhèjiā cāntīngde hǎixiān? (Does he / she like this restaurant's spring rolls?)

_____

3 Nàjiā biànlì shāngdiànde règǒu zěnmeyàng? (How are that convenience store's hot dogs?)

_____

4 Zhèjiān cānguǎnde shuǐjiǎo zěnmeyàng? (Do people like sleeping in this restaurant?)

_____

C Answer the questions using the words in parentheses.

Ex: Nǐ zuì xǐhuān chī shénme hǎixiān? (crab) → Wǒ zuì xǐhuān chī pángxiè.

1 Nǎbù chēzi bǐjiào hǎokāi? (that red car)

_____

2 Nǎtái mótuōchē zuì hǎoqí? (that green motorcycle)

_____

3 Tāmen zài cāntīngde shíhòu zuì xǐhuān chī shénme? (lobster)

_____

4 Nǐ érzide xīn wánjù zěnmeyàng? (fun)

_____

D 119.01 Fill in the blanks with the answers you hear.

1 Nàjiàn máoyī zěnmeyàng?
Nàjiàn máoyī _____.

2 Zhèshuāng xiézi zěnmeyàng?
Zhèshuāng xiézi _____.

3 Nàtái lǜsède chēzi zěnmeyàng?
Nàtái lǜsède chēzi _____.

4 Zhèjiān shāngdiàn zěnmeyàng?
Zhèjiān shāngdiàn _____.

Xiān . . . Zài . . . Ránhòu

A Match your new vocabulary words with their definitions.

1 ___ xiān		**a** breakfast
2 ___ zhé (yīfú)		**b** to turn left
3 ___ zài		**c** to walk; to go
4 ___ zǒu		**d** then; again
5 ___ ránhòu		**e** to turn
6 ___ zhízǒu		**f** lunch
7 ___ zǎofàn		**g** to turn right
8 ___ zhuǎn		**h** then; after that
9 ___ wǔfàn		**i** first
10 ___ zuǒzhuǎn		**j** dinner
11 ___ wǎnfàn		**k** to walk; (go) straight
12 ___ yòuzhuǎn		**l** to fold (clothes)

B Translate the following sentences.

Ex: Nǐ xiǎng qù nǎ lǐ chī wǎnfàn? → Where would you like to go to eat dinner?

1 Tā jǐdiǎn chī zǎofàn? _____

2 Nǐ xiàkè yǐhòu xiǎng bù xiǎng yīqǐ chī wǔfàn? _____

3 Wǒ míngtiān yào bāng wǒ māma zhé yīfú. _____

4 Nǐ bàbamāma jiā zěnme zǒu? _____

C Unscramble the following sentences.

Ex: wǒ / xǐyīdiàn / qù / zěnme / ? → Wǒ zěnme qù xǐyīdiàn?

1 zǒu / měishùguǎn / zěnme / ? _____

2 huǒchēzhàn / qù / zěnme / ? _____

3 Jiùjīnshān / zǒu / jīchǎng / zěnme / ? _____

4 nàjiā / zěnme / qù / nǐ / diànyǐngyuàn / ? _____

5 zěnme / shāngrén / nàgè / shàngbān / qù / ? _____

6 hǎochīde / nàjiān / qù / zěnme / cānguǎn / ? _____

D Are the following translations correct? Write out the correct translation if you come across any errors.

Ex: Nǐ xiān zhízǒu, zài zuǒzhuǎn, ránhòu yòuzhuǎn. (First, go straight. Then, turn right. Then, turn left.) → Incorrect – First, go straight. Then, turn left. After that, turn right.

1 Nǐ xiān zhízǒu, zài zuǒzhuǎn, ránhòu yòuzhuǎn. (First, go straight. Then, turn right. After that, turn right.)

_____

2 Nǐ xiān yòuzhuǎn, zài yòuzhuǎn, ránhòu zhízǒu. (First, turn right. Then, turn right. After that, go straight.)

_____

3 Nǐ xiān zuǒzhuǎn, zài zuǒzhuǎn, ránhòu yòuzhuǎn. (First, turn left. Then, turn right. After that, turn right.)

_____

4 Nǐ xiān yòuzhuǎn, zài zhízǒu, ránhòu zuǒzhuǎn. (First, turn right. Then, go straight. After that, turn left.)

_____

Answer Key

Lesson 61

A **1** píngbǎn diànnǎo **2** bǐjìběn **3** huā **4** bǐjìběn diànnǎo **5** zìdiǎn **6** yōupán

B **1** John yǒu shénme? John yǒu píngbǎn diànnǎo. **2** Yasmina yǒu shénme? Yasmina yǒu bǐjìběn. **3** Tom yǒu shénme? Tom yǒu huā. **4** Lily yǒu shénme? Lily yǒu bǐjìběn diànnǎo. **5** Amy yǒu shénme? Amy yǒu zìdiǎn. **6** Lisa yǒu shénme? Lisa yǒu yōupán.

C **1** bǐjìběn diànnǎo **2** zìdiǎn **3** píngbǎn diànnǎo **4** huā **5** yōupán **6** bǐjìběn

D **1** A tablet computer **2** It's old **3** Dàwèi's younger sister **4** 800 yuan

Lesson 62

A **1** c **2** a **3** f **4** b **5** d **6** g **7** e

B **1** Wǒ méi yǒu shūbāo **2** Nǐde lǎoshī yǒu mǎkèbǐ ma? **3** Lǐ Tàitai méi yǒu xiàngjī **4** Nǐde nánpéngyǒu yǒu qiānbǐ ma?

C **1** Wǒde xiǎoháizi yǒu làbǐ. **2** Méi yǒu. Mike Lǎoshī méi yǒu hóngsède mǎkèbǐ. **3** Yào. Xuéshēng yào mǎi Zhōngwén zìdiǎn. **4** Mèimeide shūbāo shì fěnhóngsè. **5** Shì. Yéyede máobǐ hěn jiù. **6** Guì. Wǒde zhàoxiàngjī hěn guì.

D **1** (Incorrect) méi **2** (Incorrect) bú **3** Correct **4** Correct

E **1** yǒu máobǐ **2** méi yǒu bǐ **3** méi yǒu xiōngdì jiěmèi **4** yǒu fěnbǐ

Lesson 63

A **1** e **2** f **3** a **4** d **5** c **6** b

B **1** Nǐde péngyǒu yǒu méi yǒu zhìnéng kǎ? / Nǐde péngyǒu yǒu zhìnéng kǎ ma? **2** Tā yǒu zhìnéng shǒujī ma? OR Tā yǒu méi yǒu zhìnéng shǒujī? **3** Nǐde shǒujī shì shénme yánsè? **4** Chōngdiànqì duōshǎo qián?

C **1** Nà shì shéide zhìnéng shǒujī? **2** Tā yào bú yào mǎi chōngdiànqì? **3** Nǐ xǐhuān wǒde shǒujīké ma? **4** Tāde diànhuà pián bù piányí?

D **1** Yǒu. Wǒ yǒu wǒde qiānbǐ. **2** Méi yǒu. Lǎoshī méi yǒu báisède fěnbǐ. **3** Lily yǒu chōngdiànqì. **4** Yǒu. Wǒ yǒu hěn piányíde shǒujī.

Lesson 64

A **1** chuízi **2** diànzuān **3** jùzi **4** mùgōng **5** jìgōng **6** bānshǒu

B **1** Wǒ bú yào yòng wǒde luósīdāo. **2** Tāmen méi yǒu hěn duō diànzuān. **3** Wǒ gēge bú shì jìgōng. **4** Mùgōng méi yǒu qiánzi.

C **1** Nǐ bàba xǐhuān tāde xīnde diànzuān ma? / Nǐ bàba xǐ bù xǐhuān tāde xīnde diànzuān? **2** Mùgōng xiǎng mài tāde jiùde gōngjù ma? / Mùgōng xiǎng bù xiǎng mài tāde jiùde gōngjù? **3** Jìgōng yǒu hěn duō bānshǒu ma? / Jìgōng yǒu méi yǒu hěn duō bānshǒu? **4** Jìgōng yǒu jùzi ma? / Jìgōng yǒu méi yǒu jùzi? **5** Wǒde gōngjù zài nǎ lǐ? **6** Nǐ(de) xiānshēngde gōngjùxiāng hěn dà ma?

D **Tools:** qiánzi, luósīdāo, jùzi, chuízi, diànzuān **School supplies:** shūbāo, kèběn, qiānbǐ, zìdiǎn **Electronic devices:** (zhào)xiàngjī, chōngdiànqì, shǒujī, bǐjìběn diànnǎo

E **1** F **2** T **3** F **4** F **5** F **6** T

Lesson 65

A **1** two daughters **2** three men **3** one child **4** ten Chinese people **5** five firefighters **6** six Americans

B **1** Yǒu. Wǒ yǒu liǎnggè érzi. **2** Yǒu. Tā yǒu sāngè nǚ'ér. **3** Méi yǒu. Tāmen méi yǒu xiǎohái. **4** Yǒu. Lǎoshī yǒu èrshíwǔgè xuéshēng. **5** Méi yǒu. Wǒ gēge méi yǒu hěn duō péngyou. **6** Méi yǒu. Ta méi yǒu xiōngdì jiěmèi.

C **1** Wǒmen yǒu wǔgè bóbo. **2** Lǎobǎn yǒu liǎnggè mìshū. / Mìshū yǒu liǎnggè lǎobǎn. **3** Yīyuàn yǒu shísāngè yīshēng. **4** Wǒ yǒu sāngè gēge.

D **1** Wǒde nǚpéngyǒu yǒu sìgè jiějie. **2** Tā bàba yǒu liǎnggè dìdi. **3** Jiàoshòu méi yǒu hěn duō xuéshēng. **4** Wǒ nǚ'ér yǒu sāngè péngyǒu.

E **1** Correct **2** He / She doesn't have your hammer. **3** Correct **4** Do these children have toys? **5** Who has a pen?

Lesson 66

A **1** jìmǔ **2** jìfù **3** érzi **4** nǚ'ér

B **1** Cāntīng yǒu jǐgè chúshī? **2** Tāmen yǒu jǐgè jiàoliàn? **3** Lín Tàitai yǒu jǐgè xiǎohái? **4** Tā yǒu jǐgè xiōngdì jiěmèi?

C **1** Tāmen yǒu jǐgè xiōngdi? **2** Wǒde jìfù zài gōngzuò. **3** Tāde jìmǔ jiào shénme míngzi? **4** Lily yǒu méi yǒu Yīngwén zìdiǎn?

D **1** Méi yǒu. Tā méi yǒu nǚpéngyǒu. **2** Yǒu. Tā yǒu liǎnggè dìdi. **3** Yǒu. Tā yǒu yīgè gēge. **4** Méi yǒu. Tāde bàbamāma méi yǒu hěn dàde fángzi.

E **1** He / She is a businessman / businesswoman. **2** The teacher has 15 students. **3** How many friends do you have? **4** Whose cell phone is this?

F Wǒ shì Alexander. Wǒ sì suì. Wǒ mèimei jiào Elia. Tā yī suì . . . (I am Alexander. I am four years old. My younger sister is (called) Elia. She is one year old . . .

Lesson 67

A **1** b **2** c **3** f **4** g **5** h **6** a **7** e **8** d

B **1** Lily zài nóngchǎng. **2** Tiānqì hěn hǎo. **3** Tā yǒu yīzhī shānyáng. **4** Tā yǒu wǔzhī jī. **5** Yǒu. Tā yǒu liǎngzhī māo. **6** (Dà.) Tāde gǒu hěn dà.

C **1** Wǒ yǒu liǎngběn Zhōngwén kèběn. **2** Nóngchǎng yǒu shísìzhī yāzi. **3** Wǒmen jiā yǒu sìzhī māo. **4** Xuéxiào yǒu èrshíqīgè lǎoshī.

D **1** Tā(de) jiā yǒu jǐkǒu rén? **2** Chǒngwùdiàn yǒu jǐzhī māo? **3** Nóngchǎng yǒu jǐzhī jī? **4** Cāntīng yǒu jǐgè chúshī? **5** Tā yǒu jǐběn Fǎwén shū?

Lesson 68

A **1** Qǐng **2** pútáojiǔ **3** píjiǔ **4** zhāng **5** lǜchá **6** xiāngbīnjiǔ

B **Alcoholic:** píjiǔ, hóngpútáojiǔ, xiāngbīnjiǔ, báipútáojiǔ **Teas:** hóngchá, lǜchá **Juices:** píngguǒzhī, chéngzhī, níngméngzhī

C **1** zhī **2** běn **3** zhāng **4** bēi / píng **5** gè **6** gè

D **1** Nǐmen xiǎng hē yībēi lǜchá ma? / Nǐmen xiǎng bù xiǎng hē yībēi lǜchá? **2** Nǐ yǒu hóngchá ma? / Nǐ yǒu méi yǒu hóngchá? **3** Nǐ xǐhuān hē pútáojiǔ ma? / Nǐ xǐ bù xǐhuān hē pútáojiǔ? **4** Tāde érzi kěyǐ hē kāfēi ma? / Tāde érzi kě bù kěyǐ hē kāfēi? **5** Tāmen yǒu jǐběn Xībānyáwén shū? **6** Nóngmín yǒu wǔzhī jī ma?/ Nóngmín yǒu méi yǒu wǔzhī jī?

E **1** Tā xǐhuān hē hóngpútáojiǔ ma? **2** Nǐmen jiā yǒu chá ma? **3** Nǐ néng bāng wǒ mǎi liǎngpíng báipútáojiǔ ma? **4** Tāmen xiǎng mǎi yīpíng shuǐ ma?

Lesson 69

A **People:** gāozhōngshēng, nánhái(zi), nǚrén, nánrén, dàxuéshēng, nǚhái(zi) **Places:** gāozhōng, xuéxiào, dàxué

B **Answers will vary.**

C **1** Nàgè gāozhōngshēng fēicháng gāo. That high school student is extremely tall. **2** Zhègè nǚrénde xiānshēng shì yáyī. / Yáyī shì zhègè nǚrénde xiānshēng. This woman's husband is a dentist. / The dentist is this woman's husband. **3** Nàgè dàxuéshēng bù xǐhuān hē píjiǔ. That college student doesn't like to drink beer. **4** Zhègè jǐngchá hěn qínláo. This police officer is very hardworking.

D **1** gāozhōngshēng **2** dàxuéshēng **3** nánháizi **4** nǚháizi

E **1** Nǐ xǐhuān zhègè lǎoshī ma? / Nǐ xǐ bù xǐhuān zhègè lǎoshī? **2** Nàgè nánrén yǒu fángzi ma? / Nàgè nánrén yǒu méi yǒu fángzi? **3** Zhègè gāozhōngshēng huì qí mótuōchē ma? / Zhègè gāozhōngshēng huì bú huì qí mótuōchē? **4** Nàgè nánháizi (hěn) guāi ma? **5** Zhègè nǚrén shì nǐde āyí ma? / Zhègè nǚrén shì bú shì nǐde āyí?

Lesson 70

A **1** yìng **2** ruǎn **3** tàng **4** cháng **5** bīng **6** zhòng

B **1** Correct – This bottle of champagne is very expensive. **2** zhī – That bear is very big. **3** Correct – I want to buy five rabbits. **4** bēi / píng – Little sister would like to drink a cup / glass of orange juice. **5** Correct – Whose chair is that? **6** Correct – That magazine is very good.

C **1** nàzhī shīzi **2** nàzhāng hěn shūfúde chuáng **3** zhèbēi kāfēi **4** nàběn Fǎwén shū **5** zhèwǎn tāng **6** zhègè gāozhōngshēng

D **1** Nàzhī tùzide ěrduō hěn cháng. **2** Nàgè rén shì tāde nánpéngyǒu ma? / Tāde nánpéngyǒu shì nàgè rén ma? **3** Xiǎoxīn! Zhèwǎn tāng hěn tàng! **4** Yīnwèi wǒde shǒu hěn bīng, suǒyǐ wǒ yào dài shǒutào. **5** Zhèběn Rìwén kèběn guì bú guì?

Lesson 71

A **1** a foreigner **2** upstairs **3** inside **4** outside **5** a room **6** downstairs

B **1** Dìdi zài tāde fángjiān ma? **2** Nǐ zài wàimiàn ma? **3** Nǐmen zài nǎ lǐ? **4** Nǐde fángjiān zài nǎ lǐ?

C **1** Nǐde lǎogōng shì bú shì wàiguórén? **2** Nǐde māo zài lóushàng ma? **3** Nǐ jiějiede fángjiān zài nǎ lǐ? **4** Tāde nánpéngyǒu zài lóuxià.

D **1** Paul is in his room. **2** Cody is downstairs. **3** Jill is upstairs. **4** Ashley is inside. **5** Robert is outside. **6** Jessica is in her mom's room.

Lesson 72

A **1** shàngmiàn **2** hòumiàn **3** qiánmiàn **4** qiángbì **5** xiàmiàn **6** lǐmiàn

B **1** Bēizi zài zhuōzide shàngmiàn. / Bēizi zài zhuōzi shàng. **2** Wǒde bǐjìběn diànnǎo zài wǒde shūbāode lǐmiàn. / Wǒde bǐjìběn diànnǎo zài wǒde shūbāo lǐ. **3** Bàbade chuízi zài gōngjùxiāngde lǐmiàn. / Bàbade chuízi zài gōngjùxiāng lǐ. **4** Dìdide zāngde yīfú zài tāde chuángde xiàmiàn. / Dìdide zāngde yīfú zài tāde chuáng xià. **5** Jiàoshòu zài nǐ(de) hòumiàn.

C **1** Hóuzi zài dòngwùyuán. **2** Zhèběn shū zài yǐzide shàngmiàn. / Zhèběn shū zài yǐzi shàng. **3** Nàzhī māo zài zhuōzide xiàmiàn. / Nàzhī māo zài zhuōzi xià. **4** Sìgè chéngzi zài bīngxiāngde lǐmiàn. / Sìgè chéngzi zài bīngxiāng lǐ. **5** Tāde wǎncān zài kǎoxiāngde lǐmiàn. / Tāde wǎncān zài kǎoxiāng lǐ. **6** Wǒ zài kètīng. **7** Shízhōng zài qiángbìde shàngmiàn. / Shízhōng zài qiángbì shàng. **8** Diànshì zài qiángbìde qiánmiàn. / Diànshì zài qiángbì qián.

D **1** Xiànzài Dàwèi zài lóushàng. **2** Zuótiān Pèishān zài tāde fángjiān. **3** Xīngqīliù Dàwèi zài cāntīngde qiánmiàn. **4** Qiántiān Pèishān zài lóuxià. **5** Xīngqīrì Dàwèi zài wàimiàn. **6** Jīntiān Pèishān zài túshūguǎnde lǐmiàn.

E Answers will vary.

Lesson 73

A 1 b 2 c 3 h 4 d 5 f 6 e 7 j 8 i 9 a 10 g

B 1 Diànyǐngyuàn zài bówùguǎnde pángbiān. 2 Túshūguǎn zài měishùguǎnde yòubiān.
3 Zhōngguó cāntīng zài jiāyóuzhànde duìmiàn. 4 Wǒ jiā zài Dàwèi jiāde pángbiān. 5 Gāozhōng zài
yóulèchǎngde zuǒbiān. 6 Jiǔbā zài biànlì shāngdiànde hòumiàn.

C 1 c 2 d 3 a 4 b

D 1 Qiúchǎng zài hǎitānde qiánmiàn ma? 2 Xǐyīdiàn zài gāozhōngde duìmiàn ma? 3 Tāde xuéxiào zài
nǎ lǐ? 4 Jiānádà zài nǎ lǐ? 5 Mòxīgē zài nǎ lǐ? 6 Nǐde nǚpéngyǒu zài bàngōngshì ma?

E Answer will vary.

Lesson 74

A 1 to wash (to take a shower) 2 Correct 3 to shave (beard) 4 to comb (hair) 5 Correct 6 to cut /
trim (hair)

B 1 Tā xiǎng qù chāojí shìchǎng. 2 Yào. Míngtiān wǒ yào jiǎn tóufǎ. 3 Wǒmen xiǎng qù dòngwùyuán.
4 Yào. Wǒ yào mǎi nàběn shū. 5 Wǒ(de) nǚ'ér yào hē yībēi guǒzhī. 6 Jīntiān tāmen xiǎng qù
hǎitān.

C 1 Míngnián nǐ xiǎng qù nǎ lǐ? 2 Jīnnián tā yào qù nǎ lǐ? 3 Nǐmen xiǎng qù nǎ lǐ? 4 Míngtiān támen
yào qù nǎ lǐ? 5 Hòutiān nǐ érzi xiǎng qù nǎ lǐ? 6 Jīntiān nǐ nǚ'ér yào qù nǎ lǐ?

D Answers will vary

E Answers will vary

Lesson 75

A 1 b 2 g 3 e 4 d 5 a 6 h 7 c 8 f

B 1 Tā xiǎng diǎn niúròu chǎofàn. 2 Wǒde fùqīn xiǎng hē báipútáojiǔ. 3 Wǒmende mǔqīn xiǎng
zuòfàn / zhǔfàn. 4 Xiǎng. Lily xiǎng hē yībēi lǜchá. 5 Hǎokàn. Nàbù diànyǐng hěn hǎokàn.
6 Bù. Zhètái diànshì bú guì.

C 1 Mìshū xiǎng zhǎo xīnde gōngzuò ma? / Mìshū xiǎng bù xiǎng zhǎo xīnde gōngzuò? 2 Nǐ xiǎng qù
hǎitān ma? / Nǐ xiǎng bù xiǎng qù hǎitān? 3 Nǐ yào mài nàtái diànnǎo ma? / Nǐ yào bú yào mài
nàtái diànnǎo? 4 Tāmen yào diǎn chūnjuǎn ma? / Tāmen yào bú yào diǎn chūnjuǎn? 5 Lǎoshī
(hěn) xiǎng tāde nǚpéngyǒu ma? / Lǎoshī xiǎng bù xiǎng tāde nǚpéngyǒu?

D 1 Chúshī yào mǎi xīnde dāozi. The chef wants to / is going to / must buy a new knife. 2 Wǒ hěn
xiǎng mǎi nàbù chēzi. I would really like to buy that car. 3 Tā bù xǐhuān zhètái diànshì. He/She
doesn't like this TV. 4 Wǒmen xiǎng diǎn sānwǎn báifàn. We would like to order three bowls of
white rice.

E 1 Tā yào (xiǎng) diǎn jīròu chǎofàn. 2 Míngtiān tā yào qù kàn yáyī. 3 Wǒmen yào shuā yá.
4 Wǒ hěn xiǎng wǒde xiānshēng (lǎogōng). 5 Tāmen xiǎng mài tāmende fángzi.

Lesson 76

A Dàwèi: **Dàhòutiān** shì wǒde shēngrì.

Pèishān: **Nǐ** jǐ suì?

Dàwèi: Wǒ shí suì. Míngtiān shì wǒde shēngrì **pàiduì**. Nǐ xiǎng lái ma?

Pèishān: Xiǎng. Wǒ xiǎng qù nǐde shēngrì pàiduì, dànshì wǒ bù néng qù.

Dàwèi: **Wèishénme**?

Pèishān: Yīnwèi míngtiān wǒ yào qù **Luòshānjī**.

Dàwèi: Wǒ hěn xǐhuān Luóshānjī yě xǐhuān **Jiùjīnshān**.

Pèishān: Wǒ yě shì. **Jiāzhōu** zhēnde hěn piàoliàng.

B **1** Correct **2** Incorrect. Can you go to Dàwèi's party? **3** Correct **4** Correct **5** Incorrect. Is this bowl of soup hot? **6** Incorrect. That black car is too expensive. **7** Correct

C **1** Nàtái bǐjìběn diànnǎo hěn hǎoyòng. **2** Zhèbù diànyǐng bú tài hǎokàn. **3** Nàxiē chūnjuǎn zhēn guì. **4** Zhèxiē bēizi tài xiǎo. **5** Zhèwǎn báifàn bù hǎochī. **6** Nàgè dàxuéshēng chāo cōngmíng.

D Answers will vary.

Lesson 77

A **1** f **2** g **3** d **4** a **5** c **6** b **7** e

B **1** c **2** b **3** a **4** d

C **1** Zhuōzi shàng yǒu liǎngtái bǐjìběn diànnǎo. **2** Nǐde chēzi lǐ yǒu hěn duō lèsè. **3** Yǐzi xià yǒu yīzhī qiānbǐ. **4** Kǎoxiāng lǐ yǒu méi yǒu miànbāo? **5** Dìtǎn shàng yǒu liǎngzhī māo. **6** Wēibōlú lǐ yǒu yīwǎn báifàn.

D **1** duōshǎo **2** jǐ **3** duōshǎo **4** jǐ **5** duōshǎo **6** jǐ

E **1** Nǐde péngyǒu jiā yǒu jǐzhī gǒu? (2) How many dogs are there in your friend's house? A: Wǒde péngyǒu jiā yǒu liǎngzhī gǒu. **2** Jiùjīnshān yǒu duōshǎo rén? (900,000) How many people are there in San Francisco? A: Jiùjīnshān yǒu 900,000 gè rén. **3** Tāmen jiā yǒu jǐtái diànshì? (3) How many televisions are there in their house? A: Tāmen jiā yǒu sāntái diànshì. **4** Wǒmende xiǎohái yǒu duōshǎo làbǐ? (64) How many crayons do your children have? A: Wǒmende xiǎohái yǒu liùshísìzhī làbǐ.

F **1** Chicago **2** Los Angeles **3** It's warm. **4** There are many museums and beautiful parks. **5** She mentions that there are a lot of beaches and famous movie stars.

Lesson 78

A **1** Tā zài pǎobù. **2** Tā zài tiàowǔ. **3** Amy zài tiào. **4** Wǒ zài chī zǎocān. **5** Tāmen zài tī zúqiú. **6** Wǒmen zài shuō / jiǎng Zhōngwén.

B **1** Nàxiē lùshī zài yùndòng. **2** Wǒ zài chuān yīfú. **3** Zhègè lǎoshī zài xiězì. **4** Lily zài wán diàndòng yóuxì. **5** Tā zài xǐzǎo. **6** Tāmen zài kàn diànyǐng.

C **1** xuéxí **2** dǎ **3** tīng **4** zuò **5** tán

D 1 Nàgè hùshì zài bāng yīshēng. / Nàgè yīshēng zài bāng hùshì. 2 Zhègè jūnrén zài pǎobù.
3 Nàgè yǎnyuán zài chī wǎncān. 4 Shéi zài kāi wǒde chē?

E 1 Preposition 2 Present Progressive 3 Preposition 4 Present Progressive 5 Present Progressive

F Answers will vary

Lesson 79

A 1 fùxí 2 xīnwén 3 zài 4 gōngzuò

B 1 Dàwèide bàba zhèng zài kàn bàozhǐ. 2 Pèishānde mèimei zhèng zài fùxí Xībānyáwén. 3 Dàwèide gēge zhèng zài chuān yīfú. 4 Pèishānde dìdi zhèng zài xǐ shǒu. 5 Dàwèide māma zhèng zài shuā yá.
6 Pèishānde jiějie zhèng zài gōngzuò.

C 1 Incorrect. I am reviewing Chinese. 2 Incorrect. His job is in New York. 3 Incorrect. Who is singing?
4 Correct. 5 Incorrect. Are they drinking green tea? 6 Incorrect. My wife is at the restaurant.

D 1 Present Progressive 2 Preposition 3 Preposition 4 Preposition 5 Present Progressive

Lesson 80

A 1 d 2 a 3 b 4 e 5 c

B Answers will vary.

C 1 Correct 2 Xiǎng 3 Correct 4 Correct 5 Gāo 6 Correct

D 1 Why don't you want to go to the party? 2 I am looking for a job. I would like to earn a lot of money. 3 May I use your tools? 4 Do they have pets? 5 Do you guys like doing the dishes?
6 Is that cup of black tea hot?

E 1 Zài. Hùshì zài yīyuàn. 2 Bú zài. Lǎobǎn bú zài bàngōngshì. 3 Shì. Wǒmen xiǎng zū gōngyù.
4 Lily yào hē pútáojiǔ. 5 Pàiduì yǒu shíliùgè rén. 6 Bù xǐhuān. Wǒde jiārén bù xǐhuān qù qiúchǎng.

Lesson 81

A 1 yèdiàn 2 chūguó 3 yóujú 4 jiàotáng 5 yàofáng 6 miànbāodiàn

B 1 We are going to go to the bakery the day after tomorrow. 2 Would you like to go to the nightclub on Saturday? 3 Are they home today? 4 Are you guys eating breakfast now? 5 Is your dad going to leave the country in June? 6 Was your wife tired yesterday?

C 1 Yàofáng zài jiàotángde duìmiàn. 2 Wǒmen xīngqīyī xiǎng qù kāfēitīng. 3 Bú zài. Xiànzài Wáng Xiānshēng bú zài yàofáng. 4 Xiǎng. Xīngqīwǔ wǒ xiǎng qù yèdiàn. 5 Tā jīntiān zài dàxué (lǐ).
6 Wǒde nǎinai zuótiān zài miànbāodiàn.

D 1 yèdiàn – Because they're bored today, they're going to go to the nightclub. 2 xiǎng – Because the teacher is in China, he/she misses his/her family. 3 yàofáng – Because he/she doesn't feel well, he/she is going to go to the pharmacy. 4 chūguó – Because it's August, everyone wants to go abroad.

E 1 She has to do homework. 2 No, she thinks the museum is boring. 3 the art gallery 4 She agrees to go to Dàwèi's house for dinner. 5 She likes to eat noodles.

Lesson 82

A 1 V 2 N 3 V 4 N 5 V 6 N 7 V 8 V 9 N 10 V 11 N

B 1 Nǐ jīntiān yào liànxí xiǎotíqín ma? OR Jīntiān nǐ yào liànxí xiǎotíqín ma? 2 Shéi huì dǎ gǔ?
3 Lily xǐ bù xǐhuān chuī lǎba? 4 Kǒuqín hěn piányí.

C 1 Huì. Mike Lǎoshī hěn huì dǎ gǔ. 2 Bù xiǎng. Wǒ bù xiǎng kàn nǐde xiǎotíqín. 3 Bú yào. Tā bú yào
mǎi xīnde lǎba. 4 Wǒmende péngyǒude gāngqín hěn guì.

D 1 Dàwèide māma huì chuī kǒuqín. 2 Dàwèide bàba yě huì chuī kǒuqín. 3 Dàwèide gēge huì tán gāngqín.
4 Dàwèide jiějie huì lā xiǎotíqín. 5 Dàwèide mèimei huì chuī lǎba. 6 Dàwèide dìdi huì dǎ gǔ.

E 1 John, nǐ huì tán jítā ma? Huì. Wǒ huì tán jítā. (John, can you play the guitar? Yes, I can play the
guitar.) Nǐ huì dǎ gǔ ma? Bú huì. Wǒ bú huì dǎ gǔ. (Can you play the drums? No, I can't. I can't
play the drums.) Nǐ xiǎng xué dǎ gǔ ma? (Would you like to learn how to play the drums?) Xiǎng.
Wǒ xiǎng xué dǎ gǔ. (Yes, I would. I would like to learn how to play the drums.) 2 Samantha, Nǐ
huì bú huì tán gāngqín? Huì. Wǒ huì tán gāngqín. Wǒ yě huì lā xiǎotíqín. (Samantha, can you play
the piano? Yes, I can play the piano. I can also play the violin.) Nǐ xiǎng bù xiǎng xué chuī lǎba?
(Would you like to learn how to play the trumpet?) Bù xiǎng. Wǒ bù xiǎng xué chuī lǎba. (No,
I wouldn't. I would not like to learn how to play the trumpet.)

Lesson 83

A 1 f 2 h 3 e 4 g 5 c 6 a 7 d 8 b

B 1 Nàgè xuéshēng qīyuè fàngjià. 2 Zhègè jiàoshòu wǔyuè fàng shǔjià. 3 Zhèxiē gāozhōngshēng
xīngqīwǔ fàng hánjià. 4 Shì. Míngtiān shì jiérì. 5 Wǒde bàbamāma wǔdiǎn bàn (wǔdiǎn sānshí fēn)
xiǎng chūmén.

C 1 jǐdiǎn 2 jǐyuè 3 jǐdiǎn 4 jǐyuè jǐhào 5 xīngqījǐ 6 jǐyuè jǐhào

D 1 What time is your dad going to leave the house? / What time does your dad have to leave the
house? 2 What month does Lily go on winter vacation? 3 What holiday does he / she like?
4 Do they like to go on summer vacation?

E Nǐ xǐhuān shénme jìjié (season)? Wǒ xǐhuān dōngtiān. Yīnwèi tiānqì hěn lěng, suǒyǐ wǒ kěyǐ chuān
hěn wēnnuǎnde wàitào. Wǒ yě kěyǐ dài hěn kě'àide shǒutào. Wǒ yě xǐhuān hē rè qiǎokèlì. Yīnwèi
wǒ shí'èryuè fàng hánjià, suǒyǐ wǒ bú yòng qù xuéxiào.

What season do you like? I like winter. Because the weather is cold, I can wear a warm coat. I can
also wear cute mittens. I also like to drink hot chocolate. Because I have winter vacation in
December, I don't have to go to school.

Lesson 84

A 1 kè 2 kāishǐ 3 shàngkè 4 xiàkè 5 shàngbān 6 táng 7 xiàbān

B 1 Bàba wǔdiǎn xiàbān. 2 Māma liùdiǎn kāishǐ zuòfàn. 3 Lisa xīngqīyī yào shàngkè. 4 Tom sāndiǎn
bàn xiàkè. 5 Nàgè shāngrén qīdiǎn shàngbān.

C 1 Nàgè nǚrén jǐdiǎn kāishǐ shàngbān? 2 Zhègè jiàoliàn xīngqījǐ xiǎng liànxí tī zúqiú? 3 Nǐmende
jiàoshòu jǐdiǎn xiàkè? 4 Lily jǐyuè yào qù Ài'ěrlán? 5 Nàxiē jǐngchá jǐdiǎn xiàbān?

D 1 Correct 2 Do you guys have to go to work the day after tomorrow? 3 Correct 4 Dàwèi has a day off on Saturday.

E Answers will vary.

Lesson 85

A 1 b 2 d 3 e 4 a 5 c

B 1 Correct 2 thirtieth (30th) 3 Correct 4 tenth (10th) 5 Correct 6 seventh (7th) 7 ninth (9th) 8 fourth (4th) 9 dì'èrshísān 10 dìshíqī 11 dì'èr 12 dìwǔshí 13 dìbāshísì 14 dìshísì

C 1 Nǐmen jīntiān yǒu jǐtáng kè? 2 Lily jīntiān yǒu wǔtáng kè. 3 Nǐ jǐdiǎn shàng tǐyù kè? 4 Wǒ nǚ'ér míngtiān yǒu Yīngwén kè.

D 1 Bù nán. Tāmende Zhōngwén kè bù nán. (It's not difficult. Their Chinese class isn't difficult.) 2 Nàgè jiàoshòu míngtiān yào shàng liǎngtáng kè. (That professor has (to attend) two classes tomorrow.) 3 Wǒmen xīngqī'èr shàng shùxué kè. (We have math class on Tuesdays.) 4 Wǒde háizi sāndiǎn xiàkè. (My child gets out of school at 3:00.) 5 Xǐhuān. Tā xǐhuān tāde diànnǎo kè. (Yes, he / she does. He / She likes his / her computer class.)

E 1 Nǐmen xiǎng kāishǐ xué Xībānyáwén ma? / Nǐmen xiǎng bù xiǎng kāishǐ xué Xībānyáwén? 2 Robert xīngqījǐ shàng diànnǎo kè? 3 Nǐ jǐdiǎn shàng shùxué kè? 4 Zuótiān tā yǒu sìtáng kè ma? 5 Nàxiē gāozhōngshēng jǐdiǎn xiàkè? 6 Nǐde xiānshēng jǐdiǎn xiàbān?

F They will see Movie 3 on Wednesday at 5 p.m.

Lesson 86

A 1 b 2 a 3 c 4 f 5 d 6 e

B 1 Dàwèi shénme shíhòu yào bìyè? 2 Pèishān shénme shíhòu yào kàn yǎnchànghuì? 3 Dàwèi míngnián xiǎng qù kàn gējù. 4 Pèishān zuótiān zài yǎnzòuhuì. 5 Dàwèi hòunián xiǎng jiéhūn. 6 Pèishān shénme shíhòu yào huí Jiānádà?

C 1 When do you start work? 2 When does Lily have a day off? 3 Is the day after tomorrow Sunday? 4 When is your son going to see the concert? 5 Because he / she graduates this year, he / she is happy.

D Answers will vary. 1 (Subject) (time) yào qù kàn yǎnchànghuì 2 (Subject) (time) yào shàngkè. 3 (Subject) (time) yào xiàkè. 4 (Subject) (time) yào jiéhūn. 5 (Subject) (me) yào huí Yīngguó.

E Answers will vary.

Lesson 87

A 1 Correct 2 yesterday morning 3 Correct 4 Correct 5 Friday evening 6 Sunday morning 7 Correct 8 September of 2015

B 1 Lily hòutiān wǎnshàng xiǎng huí Měiguó. 2 Tā érzi zǎoshàng qīdiǎn chī zǎocān. 3 Wǒ nǚ'ér wǎnshàng liùdiǎn bàn xiǎng chūfā 4 Tāmen jīnnián bāyuè yào chūguó.

C 1 Nǐ qiántiān xiàwǔ máng bù máng? 2 Nǐ bàbamāma shénme shíhòu xiǎng huíjiā? 3 Dàwèi jīntiān wǎnshàng yào qù cāntīng chīfàn ma? / Dàwèi jīntiān wǎnshàng yào bú yào qù cāntīng chīfàn? 4 Nǐ jiějie xīngqīsì wǎnshàng xiǎng zhǔ miàn ma? / Nǐ jiějie xīngqīsì wǎnshàng xiǎng bù xiǎng zhǔ miàn?

D **1** Nǐde péngyǒu **xīngqīrì** zǎoshàng yào qù jiàotáng. **2** Mike Lǎoshī **jīntiān xiàwǔ** xiǎng dǎ gǎnlǎnqiú. **3** Wǒmen **wǎnshàng jiǔdiǎn** yào qù yèdiàn. **4** Nàgè dàxuéshēng **wǎnshàng shídiǎn** qù shuìjiào. **5** Zhège háizi **zuótiān wǎnshàng** méi yǒu zuòyè. **6** Wǒ **2016 nián qīyuè** yào qù Bāxī.

Lesson 88

A **1** fēi **2** chē **3** chē **4** chē **5** jī

B **1** Huǒchēzhàn zài yínhángde pángbiān. **2** Méi yǒu. Suzy méi yǒu jīpiào. **3** Wǒ zài děng gōnggòng qìchē (gōngchē). **4** Tā xīngqīyī xiǎng zuò huǒchē qù Niǔyuē. **5** Tāmen jīntiān xiàwǔ yào shàng gōngchē. **6** Wú Xiānshēng xiǎng mǎi wǔzhāng chēpiào.

C **1** Nǐmen shénme shíhòu yào chūfā? **2** Tāmen shénme shíhòu xiǎng huí jiā? **3** Tāmende wàigōng shénme shíhòu xiǎng bānjiā? **4** Lily shénme shíhòu yào zuò fēijī qù Rìběn? **5** Wǒde chēpiào zài nǎ lǐ?

D **1** Nàzhāng chēpiào shì shéide? **2** Huǒchēzhàn dà bú dà? **3** Jīchǎng zài nǎ lǐ? **4** Nàtái bāshì hěn kuài. **5** Nǐmen jǐdiǎn shàng huǒchē?

E **1** Tā (xiàwǔ) 1 diǎn 45 fēn zuò fēijī. **2** Tā (zǎoshàng) 5 diǎn 15 fēn xià fēijī. **3** Tā (zǎoshàng) 6 diǎn 12 fēn zuò fēijī. **4** Tā (wǎnshàng) 8 diǎn xià fēijī.

Lesson 89

A **1** g **2** f **3** e **4** d **5** c **6** b **7** a

B **1** Lily xiàgèyuè yào qù Bōlán. **2** Lily zhègèxīngqīsān xiǎng qù Jiāzhōu. **3** Lily xiàgèxīngqīsì yào qù jīchǎng. **4** Lily shànggèyuè zài Luòshānjī. **5** Lily zhègèyuè yào zuò fēijī qù Ōuzhōu. **6** Lily shànggèxīngqī zài Àozhōu.

C **1** Correct **2** This woman was at church last Sunday. **3** They would like to go to Africa next month. **4** Correct

D **1** Bàba xiǎng qù Ōuzhōu. **2** Māma xiǎng qù Fēizhōu. **3** Gēge xiǎng qù Àozhōu. **4** Dìdi xiǎng qù Nán Měizhōu. **5** Jiějie xiǎng qù Yàzhōu. **6** Mèimei xiǎng qù Běi Měizhōu.

E Answers will vary.

Lesson 90

A **1** h **2** g **3** c **4** e **5** f **6** d **7** b **8** a **9** i

B **1** Wǒde nǚpéngyǒu měigèyuè xǐhuān qù dòngwùyuán. **2** Wǒ xiàgèxīngqīsì xiǎng qù pàiduì. **3** Zhègèxīngqī tiānqì hěn rè. **4** Nǐ shànggèyuè zài nǎ lǐ? **5** Nàgè xuéshēng měitiān xué Zhōngwén. **6** Wǒmen měitiān wǎnshàng chī wǎncān.

C **1** Wǒmen měitiān qù kāfēitīng hē kāfēi. **2** Tāmen měigèxīngqīwǔ wǎnshàng xǐhuān chūqù. **3** Nàgè shāngrén měigèyuè xǐhuān dǎ gāo'ěrfūqiú ma? **4** Nǐ érzi tōngcháng jǐdiǎn qǐchuáng?

D **1** Nàgè lǎoshī měigèxīngqīsān shàng shùxué ke. **2** Zhège shāngrén měitiān zǎoshàng yào zuò huǒchē qù shàngbān. **3** Wǒde xiǎohái tōngcháng zǎoshàng liùdiǎn qǐchuáng. **4** Xǐhuān. Tāmende māma xǐhuān chī nánguā. **5** Wǒ nǎinai měinián xiàtiān xǐhuān qù Déguó.

E Answers will vary.

Lesson 91

A **1** the study (n) **2** bedroom **3** living room **4** hide-and-seek **5** bathroom **6** a room **7** post office **8** bookstore

B **1** Wǒ zài wòshì shuìjiào. **2** Tā zài (fēi)jīchǎng mǎi jīpiào. **3** Wǒ bàba zài huǒchēzhàn mǎi chēpiào. **4** Xiǎoháizi zài fángzide hòumiàn wán zhuō mí cáng. **5** Tāmen zài yùshì (cèsuǒ) shū tóufǎ. **6** Nàxiē gāozhōngshēng zài túshūguǎn liànxí Zhōngwén.

C **1** Tā zài kètīng tán gāngqín. (He / She plays the piano in the living room.) **2** Nǐ érzi zài fángjiān lā xiǎotíqín ma? (Does your son play the violin in his room?) **3** Wǒ tàitai zài xǐyīfáng xǐ yīfú. (My wife does the laundry in the laundry room.) **4** Mèimei zài shūfáng zuò zuòyè ma? (Does little sister do her homework in the study?)

D **1** Tā zài gōngyuán pǎobù. **2** Tā zài kāfēitīng hē kāfēi. **3** Tā zài chúfáng zhǔfàn (zuòfàn). **4** Tā zài yùshì shuāyá.

E Answers will vary.

Lesson 92

A **1** b **2** h **3** d **4** c **5** j **6** f **7** g **8** a **9** e **10** i

B **1** Dǔchǎng zài cháguǎnde yòubiān. **2** Shìchǎng zài túshūguǎnde zuǒbiān. **3** Tíngchēchǎng zài bówùguǎnde xiàmiàn. **4** Cānguǎn zài bàngqiúchǎngde hòumiàn. **5** Cháguǎn zài dàxuéde duìmiàn. **6** Gāozhōng zài yóujúde qiánmiàn.

C **1** Wǒ xǐhuān zài shìchǎng mǎi cài. **2** Tāmen xiǎng zài cānguǎn (cāntīng) chī zǎocān. **3** Wǒmen xǐhuān zài bàngqiúchǎng dǎ bàngqiú. **4** Lily xǐhuān zài túshūguǎn xué shùxué.

D **1** These college students really like to watch movies at the movie theater. **2** Those high school students would like to eat lunch at the restaurant. **3** My car is not in the parking lot. **4** That man likes to drink green tea at the teahouse. **5** This young woman works at the post office. **6** This young man likes to do his homework in the study.

E **1** Bàngqiúchǎng zài nǎ lǐ? Tā zài wǒmen jiāde hòumiàn. **2** Lily zài nǎ lǐ mǎi cài? Tā zài shìchǎng mǎi cài. **3** Tíngchēchǎng zài nǎ lǐ? Tā zài cānguǎnde qiánmiàn. **4** Tā zài nǎ lǐ shàngbān? Tā zài lǚguǎn shàngbān.

Lesson 93

A **1** Correct **2** to grill; to barbecue **3** backyard **4** Correct **5** to work out **6** gymnasium **7** classroom **8** chess

B **1** jiànshēnfáng **2** xiàngqí **3** tǐyùguǎn **4** jiàoshì **5** hòuyuàn **6** niúpái

C **1** Mike Lǎoshī drinks cola every morning. **2** Mike Lǎoshī drinks beer every evening. **3** Mike Lǎoshī eats ice cream every day. **4** Mike Lǎoshī watches TV every afternoon. **5** Mike Lǎoshī plays video games every evening. **6–9** Answers will vary

D **1** Do you go to the gym every morning? **2** Is that steak good (tasty)? **3** Does your boyfriend know how to barbecue? **4** Is his girlfriend at the gym? **5** Is Chén Lǎoshī in his / her classroom?

Lesson 94

A 1 jiāoshū 2 lǚxíng 3 májiàng 4 tàijí 5 huāyuán 6 dìlǐkè 7 yóuyǒngchí 8 kāfēitīng 9 huáxuě

B 1 Piàoliàng (Is his / her garden beautiful?) 2 Shí diǎn (What time do you guys have geography class?) 3 Xiǎng (Would you like to play mahjong?) 4 Yào (Are they going to go to the swimming pool?) 5 Bú zài (Are you guys at the coffee shop now?) 6 Bú huì (Can his / her child(ren) ski?)

C 1 The firefighters usually like to drink coffee in the coffee shop. 2 The police officer would like to use the swimming pool at the gym next Monday. 3 That chef has to work at the restaurant every day. 4 This doctor likes to work at the hospital.

D 1 Tāmen měinián zài Fǎguó huáxuě. 2 Nàxiē dàxuéshēng měitiān wǎnshàng zài jiǔbā chī pīsà ma? 3 Wǒde wàipó měinián chūntiān zài huāyuán zhònghuā. 4 Zhègè nǚshēng xiàgèxīngqīliù yào zài wǒde shēngrì pàiduì chànggē. 5 Nàgè shāngrén tōngcháng zài lǚguǎn shuìjiào. 6 Zhèxiē nánshēng xǐhuān zài qiúchǎng pǎobù.

E Answers will vary.

Lesson 95

A 1 Gǎnēnjié 2 zúqiúchǎng 3 gāozhōng 4 mǎi 5 zuòyè 6 kāihuì 7 bàngōngshì

B 1 Wǒ měitiān xiàwǔ xǐhuān zài zúqiúchǎng tī zúqiú. 2 Nǐmen shénme shíhòu xǐhuān zài yóuyǒngchí yóuyǒng? 3 Tā jǐdiǎn yào zài gāozhōng shàng dìlǐ kè? 4 Tā měinián chūntiān zài nǎ lǐ zhònghuā?

C 1 Bàba zǎoshàng bādiǎn zài bàngōngshì kāishǐ kāihuì. 2 Māma xīngqī'èr zài chāojí shìchǎng mǎi cài. 3 Wǒ wǎnshàng liùdiǎn zài biànlì shāngdiàn mǎi dōngxī. 4 Nàgè xuéshēng wǔyuè zài xuéxiào kǎoshì.

D 1 Wǒde háizi měitiān wǎnshàng zài chúfáng xiě gōngkè. 2 Tā měigèxīngqī zài tā péngyǒu jiā kǎoròu. 3 Tāmen xīngqīsān yào zài lǚguǎn shuìjiào. 4 Māma měigèxīngqīsì zài xǐyīdiàn xǐ yīfú.

E 1 Mike Lǎoshī wakes up at 11:00 in the morning every day. 2 Mike Lǎoshī likes to work out at the gym every evening. 3 Mike Lǎoshī likes to swim at the swimming pool every Wednesday. 4 Mike Lǎoshī likes to go abroad every month. 5 Mike Lǎoshī goes to sleep at 10:00 every evening.

Lesson 96

A **Food:** pīsà, règǒu, shǔtiáo, hànbǎo, péigēn, dàn **Places:** Zhōngguóchéng, gāo'ěrfūqiúchǎng, chāojí shìchǎng, jiāyóuzhàn

B 1 Wǒ érzi xǐhuān dǎ bàngqiú hé lánqiú. 2 Nǐ yào diǎn règǒu hé hànbǎo ma? 3 Wǒ hé wǒde érzi yào qù jiāyóuzhàn. 4 Bàba xiǎng qù Yìdàlì hé Xībānyá. 5 Nǐde lǎogōng yào diǎn dàn hé shǔtiáo ma?

C 1 Gēge huì tán jítā hé gāngqín. 2 Tā jiějie xiǎng qù Táiwān hé Xīnjiāpō. 3 Mike Lǎoshī yào diǎn hànbǎo hé shǔtiáo. 4 Jack xǐhuān chī Zhōngguó cài hé Rìběn liàolǐ.

D 1 She has to work and go to school. 2 He has English class and geography class. 3 Yes, he does. He likes geography because it's fun and interesting. 4 No, she doesn't. She doesn't like geography because it's difficult and boring.

Lesson 97

A **1** b **2** e **3** d **4** c **5** a **6** g **7** f

B **1** Nǐ érzi gēn shéi chàng kǎlāOK? **2** Tā jiějie hé mèimei xǐhuān diàoyú. **3** Nàgè nǚshēng xiǎng yào diǎn péigēn gēn dàn. **4** Zhègè nánshēng gēn tā nǚpéngyǒu yào qù dǎ bǎolíngqiú.

C **1** My lawyer would like to eat white rice and vegetables. **2** My children and I would like to go grocery shopping and get gas. **3** Those high school students like playing cards and chess every afternoon. **4** Because my grandfather goes walking and running every day, he's very healthy. **5** With whom does that young woman practice Chinese? **6** This young man is going to go to the office and the soccer field.

D **1** Cānguǎnde hànbǎo gēn shǔtiáo hǎo bù hǎochī? **2** Nǐmen jǐdiǎn xiǎng qù mǎi cài hé jiāyóu? **3** Tāmen hé tāmende tóngxué wǎnshàng shíyīdiǎn yào qù yèdiàn. **4** Nàgè lǜshī gēn nàgè yáyī hěn yǒuqián.

E Answers will vary.

Lesson 98

A **1** Shèngdànshù **2** yīqǐ **3** Shèngdànjié **4** huàxué

B **1** Nǐ xiǎng yīqǐ (qù) chī wǎncān ma? OR Nǐ xiǎng bù xiǎng yīqǐ qù chī wǎncān? **2** Tāmen dōu shì dàxuéshēng. **3** Nǐ xiǎng yīqǐ qù diàoyú ma? Nǐ xiǎng bù xiǎng yīqǐ qù diàoyú? **4** Nǐmen dōu zhù (zài) Lúndūn ma? **5** Wǒmen dōu yào qù Zhōngguó. **6** Tāmen zài yīqǐ ma?

C **1** Correct **2** Correct **3** Does that young man live with his parents? **4** Correct **5** This math professor and that chemistry professor are both super smart.

D **1** Wǒmen xiǎng yīqǐ dǎ gāo'ěrfūqiú. **2** Wǒ gēn wǒde péngyǒu yào yīqǐ qù pàiduì. **3** Dàwèide mèimei hé tāde Zhōngwén lǎoshī míngtiān yào yīqǐ fùxí Zhōngwén. **4** Shì. Nàgè yáyī hé tā lǎopó dōu shì Bōlánrén.

E Answers will vary.

Lesson 99

A **1** b **2** a **3** g **4** e **5** d **6** f **7** c **8** b **9** h

B **1** Māma, Bàba, háiyǒu wǒ dōu yào (xiǎng) chī chūnjuǎn. **2** Jīntiān wǒ yào xuéxí Fǎwén, shùxué, háiyǒu huàxué. **3** Chūzūchē (Jìchéngchē) shénme shíhòu yào lái? **4** Míngtiān wǒmen yào qù hūnlǐ. **5** Hòutiān wǒ yào qù dǎ gāo'ěrfūqiú. Háiyǒu, wǒde péngyǒu hé wǒ yào yīqǐ qù kàn diànyǐng.

C **1** Wǒ gēge, jiějie háiyǒu mèimei yào zuò zhètái chūzūchē. **2** Zuótiān wǒde lǎobǎn, tāde mìshū, háiyǒu wǒde tóngshì zài gōngchǎng. **3** Tā yào diǎn chūnjuǎn, zhūròu, háiyǒu báifàn. **4** Míngtiān zǎoshàng Lily yào shàng Yīngwén, shùxué, háiyǒu diànnǎo kè.

D (Note: series of objects / subject + time expressions can be in any / reverse order) **1** Tāde wòshì yǒu chuáng, shūguì, háiyǒu diànshì. **2** Míngtiān xiàwǔ wǒ yào zuò gōngchē qù wǒde péngyǒu jiā. Háiyǒu, wǒ hé tā yào yīqǐ chī wǎncān. **3** Zuótiān wǒ xiānshēng, nǚ'ér, háiyǒu érzi dōu zài Zhōngguóchéng. **4** Nǐmen xiǎng chī Zhōngguó cài háishì Měiguó shíwù?

E Answers will vary.

Lesson 100

A 1 c 2 b 3 a 4 e 5 d 6 f 7 j 8 m 9 h 10 i 11 k 12 n 13 l 14 g

B 1 His / Her parents would like to meet his younger brother in California next fall. 2 Lily likes to play basketball with her friend(s) at the basketball court every week. 3 With whom are you going to go to the nightclub this evening? 4 I chat with my good friend at the teahouse every afternoon.

C 1 jǐyuè 2 nǎ lǐ 3 shéi 4 shéi 5 jǐdiǎn 6 xīngqījǐ

D 1 Zhège nánshēng měitiān wǎnshàng zài chúfáng gēn tā mèimei yīqǐ xǐwǎn. 2 Lilyde bàbamāma měigèxīngqītiān xiàwǔ xǐhuān zài kètīng gēn tāmende xiǎoháizi wán yóuxì. 3 Tā zài gōngchǎng shàngbān ma? 4 Correct

E Answers will vary.

Lesson 101

A 1 d 2 e 3 c 4 h 5 f 6 b 7 g 8 a

B 1 Wǒ bǐ wǒ yéye ǎi. 2 Tā bǐ tāde tóngxué qióng. 3 Wǒde gǒu bǐ tāde gǒu lǎo. 4 Nàxiē diànshì bǐ zhèxiē guì.

C 1 Her boyfriend is more handsome than this young man. 2 Lily is hungrier than I (am). 3 Little sister is thirstier than younger brother. 4 Yesterday Mom was angrier than Dad. 5 They are richer than we are. 6 That man is poorer than you guys.

D 1 Tùzi bǐ wūguī kě'ài. 2 Zhèxiē yīfú bǐ nàxiē yīfú xīn. 3 Zuò bāshì bǐ zuò fēijī màn. 4 Zhètái shǒujī bǐ wǒde hǎoyòng. 5 Nǐ bǐ wǒ bèn. 6 Mike Lǎoshīde shū bǐ nàběn Zhōngwén shū hǎokàn.

E Answers will vary.

Lesson 102

A 1 Jièzhi bǐ shǒubiǎo guì. 2 Ěrhuán bǐ yǎnjìng piányí. 3 Fēijī bǐ huǒchē kuài. 4 Jiǎotàchē (zìxíngchē) bǐ mótuōchē màn.

B 1 bǐ 2 zuì 3 zuì 4 bǐ 5 zuì 6 dànshì 7 zuì

C 1 This bowl of fried rice is tastier than that bowl of white rice. 2 Who is the richest? 3 Where is the best beach? 4 Our car is older than their car. David's car is the oldest. 5 That young man is the smartest student in my class.

D 1 shénme 2 zuì; shǒujī 3 Wèishénme; yào 4 Yào; shǒujī 5 yánsède shǒujī 6 huángsède; shǒujī zuì 7 bù; shǒujī; Lánsède bǐ huángsède hǎokàn.

E 1 a cell phone 2 No 3 yellow 4 blue

F 1 Zhètái xǐyījī zuì hǎoyòng. 2 Tāde háizi bǐ wǒde háizi guāi. Lilyde háizi zuì guāi. 3 Shēngwùxué kè bǐ huàxué kè nán. Shùxué kè zuì nán. 4 Lánméi shì zuì tiánde shuǐguǒ.

Lesson 103

A 1 f 2 e 3 b 4 c 5 a 6 h 7 g 8 d

B Answers will vary. **1** which cup of green tea . . . ? **2** which airplane ticket . . . ? **3** which piece of paper . . . ? **4** which bottle of milk . . . ? **5** which young woman . . . ? **6** which chicken . . . ? **7** which pencil . . . ? **8** which fish . . . ?

C **1** Nàbù hēisède chēzi zuì guì. **2** Lín Jiàoshòu zuì hǎo. **3** Lìshǐ kè zuì yǒuqù. **4** Wǒ 1991 nián chūshēng. **5** Wǒ bāyuè yào qù Nuówēi. **6** Zhèshuāng xiézi zuì hǎokàn.

D **1** Nǎběn Fǎwén kèběn zuì hǎokàn? **2** Nǎtái xǐwǎnjī zuì hǎoyòng? **3** Nǎzhāng chuáng zuì ruǎn? **4** Nǎzhī bǐ zuì piányí?

E Answers will vary.

Lesson 104

A **1** X **2** (běn) **3** X **4** shuāng **5** X **6** (zhī) **7** X **8** (zhī) **9** (zhāng)

B **1** bǐjiào **2** jiàn **3** bǐjiào **4** xīzhuāng **5** yángzhuāng

C **1** This fish is the longest. **2** You have a lot of sweaters. Which one is the most expensive? **3** They have two Chinese dictionaries. Which one is better (to use)? **4** My family has three cars. My dad's car is the best looking. **5** The market has bananas and apples. Which (ones) are sweeter?

D **1** Nàjiàn yángzhuāng hǎo cháng. **2** Nǎjiàn yīfú zuì shūfú? **3** Nǐde tàitai xǐhuān nǎshuāng wàzi? **4** Nàgè lǎoshī yào yòng nǎzhī báibǎnbǐ?

E **1a** Nǎtái shǒujī bǐjiào piányí? **1b** Zhètái shǒujī bǐjiào piányí. **2** Zhèjiàn chènshān bǐ nǐde chènshān hǎokàn. **3a** Nǎgè yīshēng bǐjiào hǎo? **3b** Zhègè yīshēng bǐjiào hǎo. **4a** Nǎbēi guǒzhī bǐjiào hǎohē? **4b** Nàbēi guǒzhī bǐjiào hǎohē.

Lesson 105

A **1** Āijí **2** yǐnliào **3** Yìndù **4** bǐjiào xǐhuān **5** zuì xǐhuān

B **1** Nǐmen měitiān dōu zuò shénme (yùndòng)? OR Nǐmen shénme shíhòu dǎ zhuōqiú? **2** Wáng Xiānshēng shénme shíhòu yào qù Yìndù? OR Wáng Xiānshēng míngnián xiàtiān yào qù nǎ lǐ? **3** Chén Tàitai zài nǎ lǐ hē yǐnliào? OR Chén Tàitai zài kāfēitīng zuò shénme? **4** Nǐde nǚpéngyǒu bǐjiào xǐhuān chī shénme?

C **1** He / She really likes cats but he / she prefers dogs. **2** Every Saturday I like playing ping-pong (pool) in the basement the most. **3** Do you guys prefer physical education class or biology class? **4** My good friend likes eating Indian food the best.

D Answer will vary.

Lesson 106

A 1 c 2 h 3 d 4 b 5 g 6 f 7 e 8 a

B 1 Wǒ wàigōng měitiān yùndòng. Tā fēicháng qiángzhuàng. 2 Zhègè nǚhái bù xǐhuān chīfàn. Tā hěn shòuruò. 3 Correct 4 Chuáng bǐ shāfā ruǎn. 5 Xiǎomāo xǐhuān chī yú. 6 Correct 7 Zhuōqiú bǐ bàngqiú gèng nán.

C 1 That lawyer is even richer than my dad. 2 Lily is even lazier than her classmates. 3 Chemistry is even more boring than math. 4 Hotels are even more expensive than motels. 5 That puppy is even cuter than that kitten.

D 1 Yǔmáoqiú bǐjiào (gèng) hǎowán. 2 Xiǎogǒu bǐ xiǎomāo wánpí. 3 Dàwèi hěn ǎi dànshì tā dìdi gèng ǎi. 4 Wǒmen xǐhuān chī chǎofàn kěshì wǒmen gèng xǐhuān chī chǎomiàn. 5 Nǐ bǐjiào xǐhuān hē kāfēi háishì chá?

E Answers will vary.

Lesson 107

A 1 yīyàng 2 Zhījiāgē 3 dà 4 xiǎo 5 tiáo 6 lù

B 1 zhèwǔzhī bǐ 2 zhèliǎngwǎn tāng 3 nàjiǔgè nánháizi 4 zhèshí'èrpíng píjiǔ 5 nàliǎngtiáo yú

C 1 Wǒ hé wǒde tóngxué yīyàng. 2 Zhèxiē cǎoméi gēn zhèxiē lánméi yīyàng tián. 3 Nà liǎnggè níngméng yīyàng suān. 4 Zhèsāngè rén yīyàng dà.

D 1 He / She is just like his / her mom. 2 Correct 3 Those three chemistry textbooks are equally difficult. 4 These two movies are equally interesting.

Lesson 108

A 1 which 2 comparative particle 3 even more 4 the most 5 the same 6 soccer match

B 1 Those spring rolls taste better than these (spring rolls). 2 Which shirt is the most comfortable? 3 These three young men are equally handsome. 4 Who is stronger?

C 1 Wǒmende shǒu yīyàng dà. 2 Nǐ gēn nǐde jiějie yīyàng è ma? 3 Wǒde nǚpéngyǒu bǐ wǒ gèng ǎi. 4 Kàn zúqiúsài zuì hǎowán. 5 Zhèjiàn wàitào bǐjiào wēnnuǎn. 6 Nǎpíng niúnǎi zuì piányí?

D 1 Zhèliǎngtái bǐjìběn diànnǎo yīyàng hǎoyòng ma? 2 Wǒ érzi bǐ wǒ nǚ'ér dà. 3 Zhèjiàn lánsède yángzhuāng bǐjiào hǎokàn. 4 Nàxiē nánshēng shì nǎguó rén?

Lesson 109

A 1 a 2 Wā(Ā) 3 ma 4 ne 5 de 6 ba 7 bǐ

B 1 Zhèbù diànyǐng hěn wúliáo. Wǒmen zǒu ba. 2 Xiànzài shì wǎnshàng shíyīdiǎn. Wǒmen qù shuìjiào ba. 3 Nǐ xǐ bù xǐhuān chī dàngāo? Xǐhuān a! 4 Nǐmen xīngqīliù wǎnshàng xiǎng gēn wǒ yīqǐ qù yèdiàn ma? Xiǎng a!

C **1** Wǒ érzide shēntǐ bù shūfú. Dài tā qù kàn yīshēng ba. **2** Nǐ xiǎng bù xiǎng qù kàn qiúsài? Xiǎng a!
3 Bú yào wán diàndòng yóuxì. Nǐ qù zuò nǐde zuòyè! Hǎo ba. **4** Zhè shì wǒde nǚpéngyǒu. Wā! Tā
hǎo piàoliàng a! **5** Zhètáng kè hǎo wúliáo. Wǒmen zǒu ba! **6** Yīnwèi wǒde nánpéngyǒu bù xǐhuān
xǐzǎo, suǒyǐ tā hěn chòu! Qù zhǎo xīnde ba.

D **1** Wǒmen qù mǎi yīpíng xiāngbīnjiǔ ba. **2** Wǒmen míngtiān zǎoshàng zài cāntīng chī zǎocān ba.
3 Wǒmen qù dǎ gāo'ěrfūqiú ba. **4** Wǒmen zuò fēijī qù Jiāzhōu ba.

Lesson 110

A NOTE: "huì" also means "can; know how to". **1** will (future tense) **2** to rain **3** will not **4** to snow

B **1** Hòutiān tā huì shàng shēngwùxué kè. **2** Míngnián wǒmen huì qù Yìdàlì.
3 Tāmen jīntiān wǎnshàng bú huì zài cāntīng chī wǎncān. **4** Lily xiàgè zhōumò bú huì tī zúqiú.

C **1** Tā míngnián huì bìyè ma? OR Tā míngnián huì bú huì bìyè? **2** Tāmen hòunián huì bānjiā ma? OR
Tāmen hòunián huì bú huì bānjiā? **3** Nǐmen xīngqīsān wǎnshàng huì chī shénme? **4** Nǐde xiǎoháizi
xiàgèxīngqī huì fàng shǔjià ma? OR Nǐde xiǎoháizi xiàgèxīngqī huì bú huì fàng shǔjià?

D **1** Nàge nǚshēng 2016 nián huì jiéhūn. **2** Zhège nánrén hòunián bú huì bìyè. **3** Jīntiān xiàwǔ bú huì
xiàyǔ. **4** Xiàgèxīngqīyī huì bú huì xiàxuě?

E **1** John xiàgèxīngqīliù huì zuò gōnggòng qìchē. **2** Mary xiàgèyuè huì zuò huǒchē. **3** Lily míngtiān huì
zuò chūzūchē (jìchéngchē). **4** Steve jīntiān wǎnshàng huì qí zìxíngchē (jiǎotàchē).

Lesson 111

A **1** yǐqián **2** xiànzài **3** juéde **4** xiǎng **5** zhù

B **1** Yǐqián tā zuì xǐhuān hē chéngzhī. **2** Yǐqián tāmen zài jiànshēnfáng yùndòng. **3** Yǐqián wǒmen
měinián xiàtiān qù lǚxíng. **4** Yǐqián wǒ mèimei xiǎng zhù (zài) Bālí.

C **1** Nǐ jiějie yǐqián xǐhuān dǎ yǔmáoqiú ma? OR Nǐ jiějie yǐqián xǐ bù xǐhuān dǎ yǔmáoqiú? **2** Nǐmen
yǐqián zhù (zài) nǎ lǐ? **3** Nǐ yǐqián wǎnshàng jiǔdiǎn qù shuìjiào ma? **4** Lily yǐqián hěn máng ma?

D **1** Wǒ nǚpéngyǒu yǐqián bù xiǎng jiéhūn. **2** Tā nánpéngyǒu yǐqián hěn xiǎng qù Mòxīgē.
3 Nàge nánshēng yǐqián hěn pàng. **4** Zhège nǚshēng yǐqián fēicháng shòu.

E Answers will vary.

Lesson 112

A **1** Correct **2** to get divorced **3** to become **4** to make; to do; to become **5** Correct **6** psychologist

B **1** He / She won't work in the future. **2** Are you guys going to buy a new car in the future?
3 They will live together in the future. **4** Professor Lin will look for a more expensive apartment
in the future.

C **1** Bú huì. Zhège yǎnyuán yǐhòu bú huì jiéhūn. **2** Xiǎng. Tā nǚpéngyǒu yǐhòu xiǎng dāng lǜshī.
3 Bú huì. Wǒ yǐhòu bú huì mài zhèběn shū. **4** Wǒ bàba yǐhòu xiǎng qù Nuówēi hé (gēn)
Ruìdiǎn lǚxíng.

D 1 Wǒ yǐhòu huì dài nǐ qù kàn yǎnchànghuì. **2** Wǒmen yǐhòu bú huì dài tāmen qù kàn gējù. **3** Nǐmen yǐhòu huì bú huì lái wǒmende bàngōngshì? **4** Zhèxiē lǎoshī yǐhòu huì jiāo wǒmen.

E Answers will vary.

Lesson 113

A 1 m **2** d **3** g **4** l **5** b **6** n **7** f **8** k **9** j **10** i **11** e **12** c **13** a **14** h

B 1 bàomǐhuā **2** Shànghǎi **3** tàiyáng yǎnjìng **4** huílái

C 1 When he / she is at home, he / she doesn't like doing homework. **2** When my wife and I are together, we like to listen to music. **3** They stay in motels when they travel. **4** When Mary and John eat pizza, they like to drink cola.

D Answers will vary.

Lesson 114

A 1 b **2** d **3** e **4** a **5** c

B 1 kāfēiyīn **2** huíguó **3** kāixué **4** xiǎoshí **5** rènshì

C 1 Nǐmen shàng dàxué yǐqián yào kǎoshì. (Before you guys attend college, you must take a test.) **2** Nǐmen kǎoshì yǐqián yào fùxí. (You guys must review before you take the test.) **3** Dàwèi huíguó yǐqián huì bìyè. (Dàwèi will graduate before he returns to his country.) **4** Pèishān rènshì tā lǎogōng yǐqián fēicháng nánguò. (Pèishān was extremely sad before she met her husband.)

D Note: Subjects/objects may be reversed. **1** the violin **2** the drums **3** call a taxi **4** drinking coffee and reading the newspaper

E Answers will vary.

Lesson 115

A 1 b **2** c **3** d **4** a **5** e

B 1 huàn yīfú **2** dàojiā **3** de shíhòu **4** shēng

C 1 In the future, I would like to become a firefighter. **2** After Dad arrives home, he likes to watch sports matches. **3** After women have babies, they have to rest. **4** You must change your clothes before you sleep. **5** After school starts, the students will be busy.

D Note: Subjects/objects may be reversed. **1** Zhègè dàxuéshēng kāixué yǐhòu huì kāishǐ shàng Zhōngwén kè. **2** Nàge gāozhōngshēng bìyè yǐhòu xiǎng qù Fēnlán hé Yīngguó lǚxíng. **3** Jiéhūn yǐhòu Bob hé Lisa xiǎng shēng xiǎohái. **4** Jiànshēn yǐhòu wǒ xǐhuān xǐzǎo.

E 1 Huì. Wǒmen bìyè yǐhòu huì zhǎo gōngzuò. **2** Wǒ qǐchuáng yǐhòu xǐhuān wán diàndòng yóuxì. **3** Fred chī wǎncān yǐhòu yào qù túshūguǎn. **4** Nàge yáyī xiàbān yǐhòu xǐhuān gēn tāde péngyǒu jiànmiàn.

F Answers will vary.

Lesson 116

A 1 c 2 a 3 d 4 e 5 f 6 b

B 1 How do they play badminton? 2 How do you guys cook noodles? 3 How does Teacher Li teach Chinese? 4 How do you work out?

C 1 zěnme 2 shàngbān 3 xǐ yīfú 4 xiàyǔ; pǎobù

D 1 Dìdi zuò gōngchē (gōnggòng qìchē) qù xuéxiào. 2 Gēge kāichē qù shàngbān. 3 Jiějie shàngwǎng mǎi jīpiào. 4 Wǒ kàn shū xué Rìwén.

E Answers will vary.

Lesson 117

A 1 how 2 why 3 why 4 why 5 how 6 why

B 1 Correct 2 Why aren't you guys coming to my birthday party? 3 Correct
4 Why don't they eat lobster?

C 1 Yīnwèi tā dùzi tòng. 2 Yīnwèi tā hái niánqīng. 3 Yīnwèi tā tài lǎnduò. 4 Yīnwèi wǒ bǐjiào xiǎng qù Ōuzhōu.

D 1 Yīnwèi jīntiān tā méi yǒu zuòyè (gōngkè). 2 Yīnwèi tāde yáchǐ huì tòng. 3 Yīnwèi kělè bú jiànkāng. 4 Yīnwèi jīntiān hěn lěng.

E **Suggestion 1:** Why don't you go online and use an online dictionary? **Suggestion 2:** Why don't you go to the library to use a computer? **Suggestion 3:** Why don't you go to a friend's house to use a computer? **Suggestion 4:** Why don't you buy a dictionary? **Response 1:** I don't have a computer. **Response 2:** I don't have a library card. **Response 3:** I don't have any friends. **Response 4:** I don't have any money. **SOLUTION:** Mike Lǎoshī will give the student $10 to buy a dictionary.

Lesson 118

A 1 Lín Tàitaide nǚ'ér zěnme zhème kě'ài? 2 Lǐ Xiānshēngde érzi zěnme nàme cōngmíng?
3 Mike Lǎoshī zěnme zhème qínláo? 4 Zhège zúqiúchǎng zěnme nàme dà? 5 Wǒde dùzi zěnme zhème tòng?

B 1 Nǐde nǚpéngyǒu zěnme zhème / nàme máng? 2 Tā zěnme zhème / nàme lǎnduò? 3 Nǐde nánpéngyǒu zěnme zhème / nàme xǐhuān diàoyú? 4 Nǐde bàbamāma (fùmǔ) zěnme zhème / nàme ài kàn diànshì?

C 1 Yīnwèi tā měitiān chī shǔtiáo gēn hànbǎo. 2 Yīnwèi kàn diànyǐng hěn yǒuqù. 3 Yīnwèi tā hěn xǐhuān xiǎopéngyǒu. 4 Yīnwèi wǒde chēzi hěn jiù.

D 1 Zhège nǚshēng zěnme nàme xǐhuān mǎi dōngxī? 2 Nàge nǚrén zěnme zhème ài màrén?
3 Nǐ bàba zěnme nàme xǐhuān dǎ gāo'ěrfūqiú? 4 Tā māma zěnme nàme yángé?

E Answers will vary.

Lesson 119

A **1** g **2** k **3** i **4** e **5** f **6** d **7** l **8** b **9** a **10** j **11** c **12** h

B **1** Correct **2** Does he / she like this restaurant's seafood? **3** Correct **4** How are this restaurant's Chinese dumplings?

C **1** Nàbù hóngsède chēzi bǐjiào hǎokāi. **2** Zhètái lǜsède mótuōchē zuì hǎoqí. **3** Tāmen zài cāntīngde shíhòu zuì xǐhuān chī lóngxiā. **4** Wǒ érzide xīn wánjù hěn hǎowán.

D **1** hěn ruǎn. **2** tài xiǎo. **3** bù hǎokāi. **4** hěn piányí.

Lesson 120

A **1** i **2** l **3** d **4** c **5** h **6** k **7** a **8** e **9** f **10** b **11** j **12** g

B **1** What time does he / she eat breakfast? **2** Would you like to eat lunch together after you finish class/school? **3** Tomorrow I have to (am going to) help my mom fold clothes. **4** How do you get to your parents' house?

C **1** Měishùguǎn zěnme zǒu? **2** Huǒchēzhàn zěnme qù? **3** Jiùjīnshān jīchǎng zěnme zǒu? **4** Nǐ zěnme qù nàjiā diànyǐngyuàn? **5** Nàgè shāngrén zěnme qù shàngbān? **6** Nàjiān hǎochīde cānguǎn zěnme qù?

D **1** First, go straight. Then, turn left. After that, turn right. **2** Correct **3** First, turn left. Then, turn left. After that, turn right. **4** Correct

Image credits

Illustrations